# PLAYGROUND & INDOOR GAMES

## FOR BOYS AND GIRLS.

A GAME OF MARBLES.

BROWNS' SCHOOL SERIES.

# PLAYGROUND & INDOOR GAMES

## FOR BOYS AND GIRLS.

EDITED BY

### WINIFRED WILSON,

AUTHOR OF "PHYSICAL EXERCISES FOR BOYS AND GIRLS," &C., &C.

PRYOR PUBLICATIONS

MEMBER OF
INDEPENDENT PUBLISHERS GUILD

75 Dargate Road, Yorkletts, Whitstable,
Kent CT5 3AE, England.
Tel. & Fax: (01227) 274655
Email: alan@pryor-publish.clara.net
www.pryor-publish.clara.net

Kent Exporter of the Year Awards Winner 1998

© Pryor Publications 1999

ISBN 0 946014 79 5

A full list of Titles sent free on request

First published around 1910
by A. Brown & Sons Ltd
Scholastic Publishers
5 Farringdon Avenue, E.C.
And at Hull and York

Cover Reconstruction
by Simon Scamp

Printed and bound in Great Britain by
MPG Books Ltd, Bodmin, Cornwall

# INDEX.

———

6

7

| | No. of Game. | | No. of Game. |
|---|---|---|---|
| Tawsey ... ... ... ... | 68 | Toy Symphony ... ... ... | 184 |
| Tea Party Trick ... ... ... | 174 | Trick with a Penny ... ... | 209 |
| Telephone, The ... ... ... | 177 | Tuft on the Table... ... ... | 175 |
| Thimble Game, The ... ... | 197 | Tug of War, The ... ... | 28 |
| This and That ... ... ... | 198 | Turning the Trencher ... ... | 136 |
| Thought Reading... ... ... | 157 | Turnpikes ... ... ... | 66 |
| Thought Reading Séance ... | 165 | Two in the Front... ... ... | 100 |
| Threading the Needle ... ... | 26 | | |
| Three Holes ... ... ... | 21 | Wall-flowers, a Pot of ... ... | 89 |
| Throwing Cards into a Hat ... | 201 | Waxworks... ... ... ... | 142 |
| Thumbs Up ... ... ... | 137 | Weighing ... ... ... | 98 |
| Tied Legs Race, The ... ... | 41 | Wheelbarrow Race, The ... | 39 |
| Tiggey ; or, Touch... ... ... | 47 | Windingup the Clock ... ... | 117 |
| Tip-cat ... ... ... ... | 60 | Witch and Witch's Man, The ... | 8 |
| Tip it; or, Up Jenkins ... ... | 146 | Wolf, Shepherd and Sheep, The | 105 |
| Tom Tiddler's Ground ... ... | 51 | | |
| Tournament, The... ... ... | 13 | Yankee Postman, The ... ... | 199 |
| Touch Wood ... ... ... | 36 | Yes or No ... ... ... | 168 |
| Towns ... ... ... ... | 170 | Your Left-hand Neighbour ... | 123 |

# PREFACE.

This collection is intended for the use of school children in playgrounds where the space at their command is not sufficient for the more noble pastimes, minor sports, and recreations requiring special appurtenances or fixed apparatus, such as cricket, football, bowls, tennis, rackets, croquet, quoits, skittles, ninepins and paper-chases, &c., &c.

It comprises a good variety of amusing games that may be played in the playground by boys and girls together, and some for boys only, and some for girls only.

The second part contains particulars of many others that are suitable for indoors. Some of these can be played when seated at a table. They will be found useful on wet days when outdoor games are out of the question; also for amusement in long evenings at home. Some of the games described are old-established favourites; others have not been published before. They are of diverse nationalities, and all are of easy and simple performance, being either absolutely without paraphernalia, or requiring only such handy and inexpensive accessories as a ball, a handkerchief, a piece of string, or a feather, &c. A very few of them, without any approach to legerdemain, which has not been introduced, are merely amusing tricks for the entertainment of young folks, such as "The Foot Trick," "The Surprise Party," &c. It will be found that several of the outdoor games, such as "The

B

Sea is Agitated," can be played indoors; and some of the indoor ones could with equal propriety be played outside, as the spelling games.

Cards, conundrums, chess, draughts, dominoes, halma, &c., are not included.

Teachers and others entrusted with the charge of the young, will find this work useful in the matter of suggestions whereby play-time may be pleasantly spent instead of idly wasted.

It is hoped that as physical exercise and playground recreations are now taken into official consideration as factors in the general scheme of education, it will supply a want, and find a welcome.

# PLAYGROUND GAMES
### AND
# INDOOR GAMES.

## 1. The Jolly Miller;
### or, The Miller's Grab.

THE players walk round and round in a circle of twos and twos, all save one who is in the centre, and who is the miller. They all sing the following rhyme, and when the line occurs in which it is stated that the miller makes his GRAB, the players have to try and change their partners by the outside ones moving quickly on to the outside places of those in front of them. In the break of the circle or wheel thus occurring, the miller tries to get a place as one in one of the couples; when he succeeds, the one left out becomes the miller, and the game proceeds; should he not succeed in displacing one of the others he is still the miller, and the rhyme has to be sung again as the wheel goes round once more, and at the conclusion of it he must make another effort, or GRAB, to get into the circle. The centre player remains miller until he gets in.

> There was a jolly miller,
> And he lived by himself,
> As the wheel went round he made his pelf;
> One hand in the hopper, and one in the bag,
> As the wheel went round he made his GRAB.

## 2.        Prisoner's Base, or Bars.

THIS is a favourite game for either boys or girls. If the playground is large, a portion of it must be squared off, if but small, the whole space can be used. It is requisite that one end of the ground should be marked off as the bases and bars, and the other extremity as the prisons. A line must be drawn down the centre to divide it into two distinct parts, in each end of which there is a base at one end, and a prison at the other. The players must be equally divided, and each division must have a leader or chief. Both sets must then stand in a line along their respective bases. The game begins by one player, generally called the Stag, making a dart in the direction of the prisons, shouting "Chevy" as he does so. He is immediately pursued by a player from the other base who tries to touch him. Another player from the Stag's base tries to intercept this second one, by touching him before he can reach the Stag, who turns and tries to return to his own base untouched. This sort of raid is repeated over and over again. When prisoners are taken, that is when they are touched, they have to stand in the prisons till the leaders of their respective parties come and touch them, without being touched themselves. When rescued in this manner, both leader and prisoner are allowed to return to their own bases without further touching. The prison of one set is not that which is exactly opposite to the base belonging to it, but that which is opposite to the other set, consequently the runs have to be made, not in straight lines, but slant ways across the ground, which gives the opposing players more facilities for

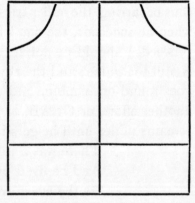

touching. The game ends when all in either side are in prison. If all are set free, it is a drawn game.

## 3.          Leap-Frog.

THERE are various ways of playing Leap-Frog, each way having a name of its own, such as "Saddle my Nag," "Jump little Nag-tail," "Fly the Garter," "Spanish Fly," &c. In every case, one set of boys bend their backs for another set to jump over. In some cases various performances are gone through in the course of the leap, such as clapping hands, waving caps, placing a handkerchief rolled up like an eel on the back of the player jumped over, and taking it off again in a return leap; and in some cases an important point is made of alighting on the right foot, and in other cases the left. The game recognised as leap-frog, is generally played by a dozen boys, more or fewer, who stand about four or five yards apart in a long row, with heads bent down so that their chins are supported on their chests, and folded arms, and their feet so planted as to make them as firm and steady as possible. One player then runs from behind, and with the help of placing his hands on the bent-down shoulders of the frog nearest him, leaps over him, runs on to the next, leaps over him too, and so on till he gets to the last when he runs a similar distance to that which is between all the other frogs, and bends his own head and shoulders down. The first one he jumped over then takes his turn, then the second, and the third and fourth, till all have had their runs and turns of being frogs. In Saddle my Nag, the leapers have to remain seated on the backs they jump over whilst they count twenty. These backs are close together like a bridge.

## 4.      The Menagerie Man.

THERE is a buyer as well as a seller. All the rest of the players are animals. The seller, who is the owner of the menagerie or museum of wild animals, places his beasts in an enclosure traced on the ground, and gives them all names, such as lion, tiger, leopard, elephant, bear, buffalo, &c. The buyer who has been out of sight, approaches the menagerie when these details are settled, and knocks at the door.

The seller asks "Who is there?"

The buyer replies "A Merchant."

The seller asks "What do you want?"

The buyer says "To buy an animal."

The seller then says "How much will you pay for it?"

The buyer replies "Ten Shillings."

The seller then says "Come in," and the buyer walks into the enclosure and asks if he has some kind of animal that he mentions. If there is one of that kind, the seller says to it "get out," and it runs away out of the enclosure. Before the buyer may run after it, he has to pay the price agreed upon by giving as many little taps on the hand of the seller, as he has mentioned shillings. He then pursues the animal he has purchased, but as it has had a good start, it often happens that it gets back again to the menagerie without being caught, when it takes another name. If caught, the buyer pretends to cut off its ears and tail with light taps on the ears and back, and he becomes a dog. When he is a dog, he has to help to catch the other animals as soon as they leave the enclosure. The game ends when all the animals have been purchased and caught, and become dogs.

# 5.   Charlie over the Water;
## or, The Royal Mail.

THE players are divided equally, and place themselves in two homes, or bays, at some distance apart. "Charlie" is stationed midway between the bays, or homes. His duty is to intercept and touch the other players as they run from one home to the other. Should he succeed, the player touched belongs to Charlie, and has to help him to catch the others as they run. They are safe in either home, but as they run across from one to the other, they are liable to be touched or caught. This game proceeds till Charlie has made them all his assistants.

| | | |
|---|---|---|
| * | | * |
| * * | * | * * |
| * * | Charlie. | * * |
| * * | | * * |

## 6. Boattie, with Fighting.

IN this game the combatants sit upon one another's feet in pairs, as in Boattie. In addition, each pair strives to enter into conflict with another, by shuffling up close to them and trying to overthrow them. They must not let go their hands or get off each others' feet. This is sometimes called a sea-fight. The players may divide into sides, and see which side makes the most conquests.

## 7. The Tail of the Wolf.

ALL the players save one, who is the Wolf, take hold of each other by their clothing, and arrange themselves one behind the other. He who is at the head of the line is the Shepherd ; he who is at the end is the Lamb; the others are the Sheep. The wolf comes to the shepherd, and tries to get hold of the lamb, who is defended by the sheep as well as the shepherd, who holds out his arms and tries to stop him, but without touching him. The sheep keep trying to get between the wolf and the lamb. When the wolf succeeds in touching the lamb, he becomes the shepherd, and the lamb becomes wolf. The shepherd then takes the second place. In this way every player is in turn, wolf, lamb, shepherd, and sheep. When the line of sheep is broken, which forms the tail, the same change is made.

## 8. The Witch and the Witch's Man.

ONE player is the witch, another the witch's man. There is a bay fixed upon in which the witch's man stands. The witch tries to catch one of the other players. When he succeeds he takes him to his man in the bay. The player who is caught, holds out his hand as far as he can reach without leaving the bay, and all the other players try to touch it, while the witch's man tries to catch them in the act. Should the players touch the prisoner, he is free. On the other hand should the witch's man touch them they become prisoners also. Both the witch and the witch's man endeavour to catch the players who endeavour to release the prisoners.

## 9.    Mount the Cuddy.

THE players, who must all be boys, divide into two parties. One party form the cuddies or donkeys. They all form a line of bent backs, supporting themselves as they bend down by clasping their knees with their hands, by which means a long narrow bridge is formed. The first player on the other side runs forward, and mounting with a leap astride the cuddies, seats himself on the furthermost. The next player does the same, and mounts immediately behind him on the back of the next boy. The rest all follow in turn. The last player, when he has mounted, must say "Mount the Cuddy" and clap his hands three times, shouting "one, two, three." The cuddies meanwhile try to throw them before they can accomplish this feat. If they fail to perform it—that is to say, if all the players do not get properly mounted to the last triumphant one at the end—they lose the game, and have to become cuddies for the others to mount.

## 10.    Sparrow Hawk.

IN this game the players are all chickens except two. These are the sparrow hawk and the hen. The chickens place themselves in a file, taking hold of one another's shoulders. The sparrow hawk and the hen circle round them. The hawk endeavours to carry off one of the chickens without being caught himself by the hen, who is in charge of them and defends them. The hawk may only walk, and never run, but the hen and chickens may run or take any pace they like, so that the chickens never leave hold of one another. Every chicken the hawk manages to seize is carried off to his nest, where it must remain till all the rest are also caught and the game comes to an end.

## 11.      Kick the Block.

FIRST of all a circle must be marked on the ground, and there must be placed in it a block of wood, or any old tin box or similar article that may be handy. They then pick out a boy by one of the counting out processes, such as—

"Inor, Minor, Mona, Mai,
Pascor, Lahra, Bonor, Bai,
Eggs, Butter, Cheese, Bread,
Stick, Stock, Stone, *Dead*."

The boy who is thus fixed upon is "he." Any boy kicks the block out of the circle as far as he can. Then "he" has to run after it. Meanwhile the others all run away and hide. "He" brings the block back and replaces it in the ring as quickly as possible, and places his foot upon it, and shouts out the names of those boys still in sight, and with the mention of each name giving a stamp with his foot upon the block. If he should have to go to look for the rest, because they have been able to hide before he called out their names, any of the others not caught and sufficiently near can rush out of their hiding places and "kick the block" out again, and return to their retreats. This feat sets those free who have been seen and named. "He" then has to pick it up once more and place it in the ring, and try again to find all the players and call out their names. The first one who is seen and named is "he" next time.

C

## 12. Ball on Horseback.

FOR this game every boy must be either mounted on the back of another, or carry another boy on his back. The ball is thrown up, and each steed tries to carry his rider so that he may catch it. The stronger boys should be picked to carry the others.

## 13. The Tournament.

THIS is a game intended for boys only. Half the boys are horses, and the other half are mounted on them pick-a-back. The strong ones should be the horses, and the light ones the riders; and care should be taken not to be too rough. When horses and riders are chosen, they divide into two parties, and arrange themselves in two lines facing each other. Each horse and man face a similar couple opposite. At a signal agreed upon, to be given by a chief properly appointed, each line moves forward, the horses throwing themselves into a gallop. The riders try to lay hold of their opponents and un- horse each other. All those who are unhorsed, are vanquished, and they are taken prisoners and their horses confiscated. The chief counts the vanquished, and when they amount to a certain number previously agreed upon, the battle is stopped and declared to be lost.

## 14. The Cap Dance.

THE boys make a pyramid of their caps. They join hands and form a circle, and dance round them. As they dance each tries to push another against the pyramid of caps. They each try to avoid touch- ing them, either by jumping over them, or striding over them, or slipping past them. Whoever is made to knock against the caps must leave the circle and take away his own cap. The game proceeds, the pyramids of caps gradually dwindling down till there is only one player left, who is the victor.

# 15.     Standall.

THE players stand in front of a wall.   One player tosses a ball up against the wall, and at the same time calls out the name of one of the other players who must endeavour to catch it.   The other players all rush away.   Directly he catches the ball he cries out, "Standall," when every player must stand motionless wherever he happens to be. He then aims the ball at one of the players.   Whoever is hit has to throw the ball.

# 16.   The Romans and the English.

## A North Country Game.

THE players, representing the Romans and the English, stand in two rows, facing each other.   A line may be drawn on the ground between them.   Each now advances up to this line and retires from it as they go through the following words :—

*Romans.*—London Bridge is broken down, for we are the Romans.

*English.*—What will you give us to mend it up ? for we are the English.

*Romans.*—We'll give you a pint of ale, for we are the Romans.

*English.*—A pint of ale wont serve us all, for we are the English.

*Romans.*—Then we'll give you a gallon of ale, for we are the Romans.

*English.*—A gallon of ale won't serve us all, for we are the English.

*Romans.*—Then we'll tell the new police, for we are the Romans.

*English.*—What care we for the new police, for we are the English.

*Romans.*—Then we'll tell the magistrates, for we are the Romans.

*English.*—What care we for the magistrates, for we are the English.

*Romans.*—Are you ready for a fight ? for we are the Romans.

*English.*—Yes, we're ready for a fight ! for we are the English.

Each player then engages with the one opposite, in the other row, and tries to pull him, or her, over the line on the ground.

## 17.     Marbles.  Odd or Even.

THERE are at least half-a-dozen games to be played with marbles. They nearly all consist of taking aim with them, either at other marbles, or at distances.  Odd or Even is one of the exceptions.  It is merely guess-work.  One player closes in his hand a certain number of marbles.  He asks his opponent, or play-fellow, whether it is an odd or an even number. When he guesses correctly he receives one of the marbles, when incorrectly he has to give one.  He then takes a handful of marbles and asks, in his turn, "Odd or Even?"  The game goes on alternately, at pleasure, or till one wins all the marbles.

## 18.     Spans and Snops.

THIS is played by one person placing a marble on the ground, and another trying to hit it with another marble, from a particular distance settled upon.  Should he succeed he wins the marble, and if his marble goes so close to the other, that he can span with his hand from one to the other, he also wins.  He then puts down a marble and the other player tries to hit it.  Every time a marble is hit or spanned, the adversary has to give one.

## 19.     Pyramids.

IN pyramids, the marbles are piled up into a cone, and a circle drawn round them.  Every time one is hit so that it rolls out of this circle, it belongs to the markman who effected the movement.  Whoever takes a shot has to pay a marble for the privilege.  Sometimes several roll out of the circle, when he has them all.

## 20.     Ring Taw.

A RING is marked on the ground.  All who are going to play put a certain number of marbles each into this pool.  The players stand round in a large circle, or line, called the offing, and take it in turns to fire with a taw at the marbles in the ring. When one hits a marble it is his, and he has a right to another turn. The players do not return to the offing, but take up their places where their marbles fall, or rest. Should a taw remain in the ring its owner is out, and if he should have won any marbles he must put them all back in the pool. And a player is also out, if his taw should be struck by any other taw, and he has to give up any marbles he may have won, to the owner of the taw. The "taw" means the particular marble with which the shots are made.

## 21.                    Three Holes.

A LINE is first drawn, then two yards from it a small hole is scooped out, and about a yard and a half from that a second one is made, and at the same distance from that, a third. The game begins by the first player trying to shoot a marble from the line where he stands, into the first hole. Should he succeed, he has the right to shoot again at the distance of a span. Should he fail, the next player begins, so they go on alternately, till one gets into the last hole. Some authorities require that the holes should be reached in this order:— first, second, third; second, first; second, third. The loser sometimes has his knuckles fired at by the winner. He places them down at the first hole, and the winner has three shots at him, from the place where his marble rests.

## 22.                    The Serpent.

EACH player ties his handkerchief into an eel, with a knot. To see who shall play first, they form a line, and stoop and throw their handkerchiefs between their legs in such a manner as it passes over their heads, too. He who throws his handkerchief the farthest is the one to begin, and the rest follow according to the distances they have thrown. This matter arranged, they untie their handkerchiefs and place them on the ground at intervals, rolled up like eels, or serpents. The first player begins by jumping successively over the handkerchiefs on one leg in coming and going. Then he passes in and out all along the line, and if in the course of these feats he touches either of the handkerchiefs, he has to put it straight and place his own at the end, and thus becomes the last boy. The second then has his turn; and then the third. Those who perform the serpentine feat without disarranging the handkerchiefs are the victors. He who remains last is the loser and must pass between two lines of victors, who may strike him with their handkerchiefs done up as eels, without knots in them.

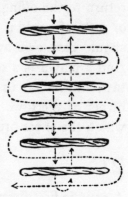

## 23. Counting-out Rhymes.

1, 2, 3, 4, 5, 6, 7,
All good children go to heaven,
When their sins are all forgiven.

1, 2, 3, 4, 5, 6, 7,
Penny on the water, twopence on the sea,
Threepence on the railway, out goes she.

### Another Counting-out Rhyme.

One-ery, two-ery, tick-ery, seven,
Eight-ery, Nine-ery, ten-ry, Eleven,
Pip, pop, must be done,
Nick-abo, Nock-abo, Twenty-one.

## 24. Mantu-marily.

PLAYERS form a ring and go round and round singing :—

Work, boys, work, and be contented,
As long as you will have to grind a mill,
For the Mantu-marily will be welcome by-and-bye,
If you'll only put your shoulders to the wheel.

They then choose partners, turn them round, and re-form the ring, going round as before.

## 25. How many Miles to Bamborough?

THIS is a Northumbrian game. The players stand in a semi-circle with their hands joined, and with two elder players at the two ends. One of these end players asks the other at the opposite side, "How many miles to Bamborough?" The other replies, "Three score and ten." "Can I get there by candle-light?" is the next question. The other replies, again, "Yes, and back again." The first then says, "Open the gate and wise us through." The other replies, "Not without a back and a bow." They all bend back, crying "There's the back," and then all bend forward adding, "and there's the bow.' The first re-demands, "Open the gate and wise us through." The two end players at one extremity then raise their hands and form an arch, under which the players led by the two elders at the other end all pass, without letting go of hands, which also  necessitates the two forming the bridge, or arch, turning inwards and passing under their own raised arms. They resume their former position, and the questions are asked by the leaders of the opposing party, and the game proceeds as before.

## 26.  Threading the Needle.

IN some parts of the country a similar game is called Threading the Needle. All the players join hands, and the two outside ones ask and reply as follows:—"How many miles to Babylon?" "Three score and ten." "Can I get there by candle-light?" "Yes, and back again." "Then open the gates without more ado, and let the King and his men pass through." Upon this, two players at one end raise up their arms in an archway, and the other leader from the other side, heads all the others who pass under the arch, or thread the needle, without letting go their hands. The same questions are asked again, only the player who asked first, replies the second time.

## 27.        The Sculptor.

ONE player is chosen, by lot or otherwise, to be the Sculptor, or Statuary. He chooses three of the other players to be statues. All the rest form a circle round them, and dance round and round. The sculptor arranges his statues in different attitudes and occupations. For instance, he makes one sit down and be a tailor, another a carpenter with a plane, and the third a musician with a guitar. He then says to the players who are dancing round, that he is going into the town, and that he has told the statues not to move. Directly he has gone away the statues jump up and dance and sing with the rest, "He is gone, he is gone." After a minute or so they ask, "Is he far? is he far?" And the others reply, "No, he is here, he is here," just as the sculptor comes running back. His statues try to resume their attitudes and places before he can touch them; but if he can touch either of them before they can do so, that one becomes the sculptor, and the former sculptor joins the ring. There must be new attitudes at every change of sculptor.

## 28.        The Tug of War;

### or, French and English.

THE tug of war is the old trial of strength that used to be called French and English. A line is drawn on the ground. The players divide themselves into two equal parties, and each party takes hold of the opposite ends of a rope, which they lift up over the mark on the ground. When every member of the party has a firm grip of the rope, they begin to tug, till one side tugs the other over the mark. A signal that is agreed upon beforehand is generally given for the tug to begin. Those who pull the other side over are the victors, of course.

## 29. Dicky, Dicky, Shine the Lantern.

THIS is a game to be played just as it is getting dark, in the open-air. The leader has a small lantern in which there is a light. The rest of the players have to catch him. He shows the light, and as they all run towards him, he turns the dark side of his lantern to them, and nimbly moves away. As they are all, literally, in the dark as to his whereabouts, they call out "Dicky, Dicky, shine the lantern." He shows the light again, and once more they run towards him, when he evades them as before. This is kept up till he is caught, and then the player who has succeeded in catching him has the lantern, and the fun continues.

## 30. Blindman's-buff Reversed.

THE well-known and much appreciated game of Blindman's-buff is extremely amusing if played in the reverse manner. Instead of one player being blind-folded, and all the others evading his touch and trying to keep from being caught by him, all the players are blind-folded except one. The fun consists in the attempts of the blind-folded performers to catch that one. They keep catching each other instead. He must run in and out, and give them plenty of opportunities to take hold of him, by gently touching them on the shoulder and mentioning their names; but he must also nimbly avoid being caught as long as he is able to do so. When effectually seized he has one more chance of escape if his captor should make a wrong guess as to his identity, by fancying he has got hold of a blind-folded comrade. When caught and named he has to be blind-folded, and the player who caught him takes his place, with his eyes open.

## 31. Hattie.

THE players arrange their hats or caps in a line on the ground in front of the playground wall. The players all stand at a given distance

D

from the hats. One of them throws a ball into one of the hats. All the rest rush away, except the one to whom the hat belongs, who darts forward, picks the ball up, and endeavours to hit one of the other players with it before they have disappeared. If he cannot hit a player, *one* against him is scored. If he should hit one, he is exempt from this score. If one should be hit, that one is to toss the ball into a hat next time. If he should miss everybody, he must toss the ball again into one of the hats himself, and try once more to hit one of the others with it after picking it up. Whoever has the lowest score at the end of the game is the winner.

## 32. Hare and Hounds.

THE players are arranged in two parties. Those on one side are hares ; those on the other are hounds. The hares are allowed a certain time to hide in, not in one party, but scattered about wher ever they can find a retreat. When this time expires the hounds set out, independently of each other, to find and catch them. When a hound succeeds in finding and seizing a hare, he has to clap him three times on the head when he becomes a hound and must help to look for the rest. The game continues till all the hares are found and turned into hounds.

## 33. Cuddy.

ONE player is the Cuddy. Whoever he catches also becomes a cuddy, and they have to join hands and continue to try to catch the others until they are all caught and have become cuddies. As each one is caught he has to join hands with the other cuddies. They all run in a line, hand-in-hand till the last one is caught.

## 34. French Tiggy.

THE pursuer's hands are tied behind his back, and he has to catch his opponents when handicapped in that manner.

## 35.   The Cat and Mouse.

THERE are two camps in this game, that of the cat and that of the mouse.   Midway, a peg is driven into the ground with a long and short cord attached to it.   When it is settled (either by choice, or lot, or counting out), who is to be cat and who is to be mouse, they are both blind-folded and the end of the long cord is given to the cat, and that of the short one to the mouse.   The game consists in the efforts of the cat to catch the mouse.   They may both move about as much as they like, but neither must let go of their cords.   The respective camps, or sides, to which they belong cheer them on, or warn them off.   The players on the cat's side mew to invite her to advance in the direction of the mouse.   Those on the side of the mouse squeak to warn it of danger.   If the cat should get hold of the mouse, she wins; but if not, at the end of a time agreed upon, they are both replaced by two of their comrades, one from each side. The game continues till all have been either cat or mouse.

## 36.     Touch Wood.

TOUCH WOOD resembles Tiggy, or Touch, with the additional feature that, if any of the players who are being pursued can touch wood, they cannot be taken prisoners.   A door, or gate, or tree, or anything that is made of wood, forms a place of refuge for them as long as they are touching it.   Directly they take their hands off it they are liable to be captured.   Sometimes iron is substituted for wood by agreement.

## 37.     The Cat Tiggy.

THE players arrange themselves in a circle.   At the cry, " The last perched is it," all seek to perch themselves—that is to say, to get their feet off the ground.   They may stand on any piece of wood, or tree, or wall, or gate-bar, so that their feet are not touching the ground. He who is the last to climb or perch himself is the cat. The players change their perches at their pleasure, and the cat has to try and catch them as they do so before they can re-perch themselves. If he should succeed, the one who is caught becomes cat in his turn. The new cat cannot touch the last one till he has been perched once. During the time the players are perched, they are safe, and cannot be touched.

## 38. The Flower-pot.

TAKE a flower-pot, into which all the players must put a forfeit of trifling value, such as a marble. Place the pot either on the ground, or on a brick, or box. At a good distance from it, make a mark of departure. When it is settled who is to begin, the first player is blindfolded, and a stick is given to him. He is placed at the point of departure, and then walked about a little so as to confuse him as to his exact position, and then he is set free and told to try and find the flower-pot and break it. He goes about feeling this way and that way with his stick for it. When he finds it, he has the right to strike three times. Should he succeed in knocking it down or breaking it, he is entitled to the forfeits, if not, the same arrangement holds good for a second player.

## 39. The Wheelbarrow Race.

THE wheelbarrows are boys on their hands and knees. They are ranged in a line in the playground, with another boy standing behind each one. At a concerted signal, each of these last-named boys lifts up the feet of the boy on his hands and knees before him, and pushes him along, by making him walk on his hands, like a wheelbarrow. The one who gets his living wheelbarrow past the winning post, or point, first, of course is the winner. The distance must not be too great. A line drawn on the ground makes as good a " post " as needs be had. There must be an umpire and a starter.

# 40. The Sack Race.

ANOTHER race is the Sack Race, in which each boy's two feet are tied up in a sack or strong bag. All the competitors stand in a line, and start at a given signal. The first to arrive at the goal selected is the winner. If there should be no sacks at hand, the knees may be tied together with handkerchiefs, which will answer the purpose nearly as well.

# 41. The Tied Legs Race.

THIS is a race run in couples, the right leg of one boy being tied to the left of another, so that they must move in concert. Directly the signal to start is given, off they must go in the direction of the goal, and the two who get there first are the winners. It frequently happens that those who are hurrying to be first meet with casualties that enable those who are moving at a slower pace to get before them.

# 42. The Potato Race.

THE Potato Race is very amusing. Should potatoes be difficult to get, balls may be substituted; but potatoes are better. There can be only two competitors at a time, who, in their turn, are succeeded by two others. The rest of the company look on. Two rows of potatoes, with a dozen in each row, are placed on the ground, about three or four feet apart, and a basket is placed midway between them at one of the extremities. The race consists in being the first to pick up the potatoes in either of the rows with a teaspoon and deposit them in the basket, without touching them with the fingers. The competitors are cheered and jeered by the spectators. It is difficult to get the potatoes on to the spoons, and then it is a feat to run with them to the basket without dropping them by the way. When they fall off the spoon, they must be picked up again by it, without touching them with the hand, as before.   As stated, the player who gets his dozen potatoes picked up and deposited in the basket before the other one is able to do so has won the race.   Two more competitors then commence the same process, when the potatoes have been placed in two rows again.   Sometimes a score is preferred to a dozen.

## 43.   The Ring Game.

A LARGE circular track must be marked on the playground with a stick for this game.   The players run round and round on this track,

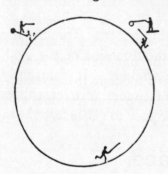

and, in doing so, without stopping, try to put a stick or rod through a ring held on the end of a stick or wire by another player. This last-mentioned boy must take care to keep at a sufficient distance not to be hit by the players in their efforts to take the ring off.   It is well to have as many rings as there are players, or nearly so, because as each ring is knocked off it rolls away, and

there would be an undesirable delay before it could be replaced for the next comer.

## 44.   The Great Mogul.

ONE player stands on a stool, or anything that will form a throne. The other players pass before this throne, one by one.   Each player stops in turn before the throne, and, addressing the performer upon it, must say "Great Mogul, I adore thee, I worship thee and bow down before thee," in the most solemn fashion.   The player personating the Great Mogul makes the most ugly faces and performs the most grotesque duties to make him laugh.   Should he succeed in upsetting the gravity of the subject, the player who laughs succeeds him as Great Mogul, or else pays a forfeit.

## 45.  Drop the Handkerchief.

A RING is formed, with one player left outside of it.   This player has a handkerchief in his hand with a knot tied in it.   He, or she, walks round the circle, touching some of the players on the back with the knotted end of the handkerchief.   He eventually drops it behind a player, who, when he finds it, has to pick it up and chase the first player round and round, outside and under the joined hands of the others, till he is able to touch him with the knot in it.   Upon being hit, the first player is allowed to unlink the hands of two others and insert himself in the ring.   The second player—that is to say, the one who has just been chasing the first one—then goes round the outside of the ring, and ultimately drops the handkerchief behind some one else.   Everyone must keep a sharp lookout to see where the handkerchief is dropped, and pick it up and pursue the one who dropped it immediately.

## 46.  Puss in the Corner.

FOUR players take up positions in four corners, and a fifth stands in the centre of this square.   Those in the corners endeavour to change places, and call "Puss, puss," to attract each other's attention when they think there is an opportunity to do so.   Directly they leave their corners to change places, the player in the centre tries to take possession of one of them.   The original owners of them either rush back into them, to await a better chance, or the puss with whom they are exchanging puts on an extra speed to try to get into it first. When the fifth player, or puss, gets into a corner at last, the one who has been displaced has to be in the centre till, in turn, someone else is displaced.   At every movement, there is always a call of " Puss, puss."   This is played by both boys and girls.

## 47. Tiggy, or Touch.

THIS is one player against any number. He has to try to touch either of the others, who in their turn try not to be touched by running from him and round and round him, but always keeping out of his reach. Directly one is touched, he becomes the pursuer, and the former joins the band against him. Some players do not allow a touch of the faces or hands of opponents to count, declaring that "flesh is free," and require the clothing to be touched. This point should be settled before beginning.

## 48. Cross Tiggy.

IN this game, when the player appointed to touch the others is endeavouring to do so, if any other player crosses between him and the person he is pursuing, he relinquishes his original pursuit to follow the player who has crossed the path. And if a second player should intervene, the pursuit is then transferred, again, to this new comer; and so on, till one is eventually touched.

## 49. Hop Tiggy.

THIS is the same as Tiggy, only it must be carried out hopping. Directly both feet touch the ground, the player must return to his starting place and begin again.

## 50. Boattie.

Two boys sit down on each other's feet, facing each other and dragging their feet back with their comrades upon them. They take hold of each other's hands for oars, and they imitate the motion of rowing by alternately drawing back their feet and arms, and propelling themselves along.

# 51.    Tom Tiddler's Ground.

THIS is something like Prisoner's Base, only less complicated.  A line is drawn to separate Tom Tiddler's ground from the rest of the playground.  Tom Tiddler takes up his position on his own ground, and tries to touch anyone who intrudes upon it.  Any player he succeeds in touching when on his ground becomes his prisoner, and has to stand behind him, and wait there till a comrade comes and touches him without being touched by Tom Tiddler.  On every occasion that a player gets the chance of taking a run on Tom Tiddler's ground, he shouts, "Here I am on Tom Tiddler's ground," to attract his attention.  When there is a prisoner to be rescued, two or th:ee generally invade his territory at the same time, and while he is pursuing one of them the others contrive to release the prisoner by touching him.  Should they be touched by Tom Tiddler in the course of the rescue, they become prisoners likewise.

# 52.    The Butcher, the Shepherd, and the Sheep.

ONE player is chosen to be the butcher, another to be the shepherd, and a third to be a ram.  All the rest are sheep.  The butcher advances towards the shepherd and asks to buy a sheep.  They look at all the sheep, and proceed to weigh them, honey-pot fashion.  He decides to buy them all.  That done, he pretends he has some other business to do, and promises he will return and pay for the flock in a short time.  Directly he is gone the shepherd drives all the sheep into a fold, which must be a large square marked on the ground.  The sheep place themselves all behind the ram in the fold, and the shepherd stands just outside it.  The butcher returns, and pays the shepherd the price they have agreed upon.  Then he asks for the sheep.  The shepherd points to them in the fold, and says he may

E

take them. He enters the fold and approaches the sheep, when the ram bars the way. If he goes to the right, the sheep run to the left, always defended by the ram; and if he turns to the right, they run to the left, with the ram still protecting them. This goes on till he is able to touch first one sheep and then another, till they are all conducted, one by one, out of the fold. The game finishes when all are taken.

## 53.     Oranges and Lemons.

Two members of the party take hold of hands, facing each other One agrees to be oranges, and the other lemons. The rest of the party form a long line in a file, holding each other's dresses or shoulders. The two first-mentioned hold up their hands to form an archway, and the rest all run through it, singing as they run—

Oranges and lemons, say the bells of St. Clement's;
You owe me five farthings, say the bells of St. Martin;
When will you pay me? say the bells of Old Bailey.
I do not know, says the big bell of Bow.
Here comes a candle to light you to bed!
Here comes a chopper to chop off your head!

At the word "head," the archway descends and clasps the head of the player passing through at the moment. He, or she, is then asked in a whisper, "Which will you be, an orange or a lemon?" without being told which is represented by the respective parties. Supposing he chooses to be an orange, he is told to retire behind the one who has agreed to be oranges; and, of course, if he should choose to be a lemon, he must retire behind the one who represents lemons. The song then recommences, and the players file through the archway made by the upraised hands as before, and the chopper descends and captures another victim, who is offered the same choice. When this has been repeated till the long file has been divided into two parties, a tug-of-war takes place. Each individual in the two lines holds tight to the next by putting his arms round his or her waist. A line is drawn, against which the leaders put their feet, and the aim for either column is to pull the other over this line.

## 54. London Bridge.

"LONDON Bridge is broken down" is similar to the above, with the exception of the words, which run to the following effect :—

> London Bridge is broken down;
>     Dance o'er, my Lady Lee.
> London Bridge is broken down
>     With a gay lady.
>
> How shall we build it up again?
>     Dance o'er, my Lady Lee.
> How shall we build it up again?
>     With a gay lady.
>
> \*     \*     \*     \*     \*     \*     \*
>
> Build it up with stone so strong;
>     Dance o'er, my Lady Lee.
> Huzza! 'twill last for ages long
>     With a gay lady.

There are various versions, and one ends, "And off to prison you must go, my fair lady."

## 55.  Night and Day.

THIS is a French variation of a familiar game.  The players divide
into two sides, or camps, one being Night, the other Day.  They
have at one end of the playground a refuge for each side.  At equal
distances from these two refuges stands a chief, or leader.  Five
steps from him on either side the players of each party form a row
with their backs turned to him, each being nearest to the refuge that
belongs to them.  The leader throws into the air a hoop which is
covered with paper, white on one side and black on the other.  If the
hoop, in falling, should show the white side, he calls out "Day."  If
the dark side should show, he calls out "Night."  At the cry "Day,"
those who are on the Day side begin to run to their refuge, which
ought to be a good distance away.  The others of the opposite
side run after them, and try to take them by touching them.
Whoever is touched is brought into the opposite camp.  The same
holds good at the cry of "Night."  The game concludes when all
the players find themselves in one camp.

## 56.  My Mother has gone to Market.

FIRST of all a "home" is made.  One player is the mother, all the
rest are children.  The mother says, "I am going to the market.
You must be very good whilst I am gone," and then she gives everyone a task.  She tells one to clean the boots (who immediately begins
to clean invisible boots), another to wash (who begins to wash
invisible articles), a third to iron (who pretends to iron), a fourth to
chop up wood (who begins to chop without a chopper), a fifth to
mind the baby (who immediately rocks an invisible cradle), and so
on till all are occupied.  Seeing them all at work, she departs for
market.  No sooner is her back turned than they all cease working
and quietly follow her, mimicking her as she goes.  She turns round
suddenly, and finds them close behind.  She exclaims, "Oh! you

naughty children," and rushes after them as they fly helter-skelter home. Should she catch any of them before they reach the home, she puts them in a corner, to remain there till the game is over. The mother once more starts for market, when the same proceedings take place, both with regard to setting tasks to all the players and their mimicry after her departure. She can vary the tasks at discretion.

## 57.    The Giant Snowball.

AFTER a large fall of snow, it is easy to make a big snowball. A small one is made to begin with, and then rolled about in fresh snow and pressed smooth all round till it gets larger and larger, and gradually becomes a giant's snowball.

## 58.    Snow Statues.

WHEN the snow is on the ground, advantage can be taken of its plastic properties to make snow statues. A white polar bear, for instance, is easily made, and is a source of much interest. Make the body first, then the head, then the ears. Put in two stones for the eyes, and get short sticks for the feet, which you must cover with snow; and finally add a tail. If you choose a sitting posture for the bear, he will require but two paws.

A snow man is another source of unfailing interest. Begin with the two legs. When these two columns are of a sufficient height, bridge them together and build the body on them, and place the head on the top of that. A cocked hat has a good effect. A snow lady with a long train has also been much admired. Where there is plenty of snow and plenty of room, a group of snow statues has a fine effect. The marriage of the snow king to the ice queen affords a good opening for any plastic skill there may be among the players. A snow cat or dog show also keeps several pairs of hands employed.

# 59. Hopscotch.

HOPSCOTCH is a game that appears to be played all over the world with slight modifications, and under various names. In Northumberland it is called hitchey-bet. In all cases a diagram, divided into several parts, is drawn upon the ground. In some places this is of an oblong form; in the North of Scotland it is circular. The aim of the game is to throw a piece of tile, or oyster shell, or some other article of similar size and slipperiness, into one of the compartments of the diagram, and hop after it and kick it successively from one to the other without letting the raised foot touch the ground, and without letting the tile or shell go outside of the marks. When either of these mishaps happens, the player is "out" and the next one has a turn. Fig. No. 1 is the kind of diagram used for this simple form. The player begins by kicking the shell into 1, thence to 2, thence

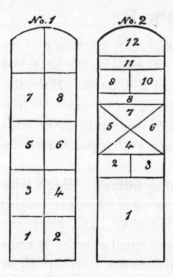

crosses over to 3, and then into 4, thence crosses into 5, and goes on to 6, and thence crosses to 7, and then gets to 8, when he is a conqueror. It requires considerable practice to achieve this simple feat on one foot. The other diagram is used in a more elaborate form of the game. Every time the tile has to be kicked home, and then pitched into the next compartment, and kicked gradually home through them all in succession. From 1 it has to be pitched to 2, and then kicked back home. It is then pitched into 3, and has to be kicked back through 2 and 1 home.

It is then pitched into 4, and has to be kicked back through 3, 2, and 1. When the player has got as far as 7, he may rest his feet, one in 5, the other in 6, before going on. The narrow compartments are difficult to hit, as the tile is apt to go short or too far, and this throws the player out.

## 60. Tip-cat.

TIP-CAT is still a favourite game, perhaps on account of the charm that a certain amount of danger gives it. The cat consists of a piece of wood, pointed at both ends. A circle is drawn on the ground, and the cat placed in the centre of it. The first player takes a stick and kneels down by the side of the cat, and strikes it gently on one end. All the other players stand round and watch for the cat. When it is thus struck it flies up, and it is the first player's business to hit it again, when it is in the air, as hard as he can. When it falls, one of the others who are looking on picks it up and throws it back into the circle. The first player then has to intercept it and knock it away. Should it fall in the circle, he must give up his place, and a second player enters the circle with the cat and sends it flying in its turn.

## 61. The Miller and his Boy.

EVERY boy should have a whistle for this game. They form a circle round two boys, who represent the miller and the boy, and who are both blindfolded. The miller, whose name is John, has a handkerchief with a knot in it. His boy, whose name is James, stands five steps in front of him. There must be a leader; and it depends upon him to make the game lively. He must point to one of the players, who is to whistle. Directly he hears the whistle, James makes towards the place whence he heard it, and his master follows and tries to hit him with his knotted handkerchief, and just as he is about to do so, the leader points to another boy to whistle. At this sound in a fresh direction, James changes his course and John follows him, and the game goes on till he actually strikes him. From time to time the leader calls out, "This way, John," or "This way, James," and then he orders a fresh whistle to puzzle them both. When James has been struck, or touched, by the miller (John), the latter is set free, and James becomes the miller, and another player takes the part of James.

## 62.

# Kites.

THE making of a kite is of as much interest as the flying of one; and it is a simple matter. Two thin, flat pieces of wood, or laths, and a piece of cane, with some string and paper, are all the materials required. One lath forms the centre of the kite, and the shorter one the crosspiece; the piece of cane forms the rounded top. The centre of this last has to be fastened to the lath at the top of it, and the two ends of it, notched, are bowed down and also fixed by a string to the crossway lath; and a second length of string goes up from one end of the bent cane to the centre of the top and down again to the other end of it. From this point it must descend to the very end of the lath, in a point, and be fastened in a notch that must be made there, and then rise up again on the other side to the other end of the bow, whence it must descend again to be fixed in another notch in the lath that is rather lower than midway down it, and then fastened to the corresponding end of the bow on the other side. Thus made firm with string in this manner, all that remains is to cover it with paper. Wings or paper tassels must be placed at the extremities of the cane bow, and a grand tail attached to the lowest point. Two holes must be pierced through the lath for the string to be made fast, and then nothing is wanted but a pleasant breeze and a summer's evening to fly it in. Authorities state that the tail should be about a dozen times as long as the kite. The crossway lath is not shown in the diagram.

## 63.    Hide and Seek.

HIDE and Seek may be played either with hiding any article that may be agreed upon, or with the players hiding one from another. In the first form, it is customary for the player who has hidden the article to help the seekers, by telling them whether they are hot or cold. When they are near the hidden article he must tell them they are hot, and when they are far from it that they are cold, and when they retreat from it they are getting cold. Whichever of the party finds the article has the privilege of hiding it next time. When one of the players is hid, the one who finds him has to hide next time. This second form involves moving about more than the first form, which can be quietly played in a room.

## 64.    A Blindfolded Quadrille.

FOUR Couples stand up in a Quadrille, all blindfolded, and go through the figures regularly to whatever music can be improvised, comb music being always possible as a last resource, when no better instrument is available. The departures and variations they all make, in consequence of being blindfolded, are a fund of amusement to the bystanders and all concerned. A mouth organ, a Jew's harp, or a penny whistle might be used, or the dancers might sing some popular tunes.

## 65.    I Spy.

I SPY is something like Hide and Seek, with the addition of a bay. All the players except one, hide. When he goes out of the bay to look for any of the others, they try to get into it during his absence without letting him be aware of their intention. If one or more should get into the bay before he observes him, or them, he must still be the seeker. Should he observe the approach of any of the players who have been hiding, he must call out "I spy," and mention the name of the one he detects first, when that player must become the seeker, and he joins the set who hide.

F

## 66. Turnpikes.

THERE must be two rows of large stones placed at intervals; these are the Turnpikes, and each has a keeper. The players must make their hoops, which represent horses, wheel between the stones in and out of all of them without touching them. One is a leader, the rest follow him. If they pass all the stones without touching them, the turnpike keepers must pay them a stone each, but if they touch any of them they have to pay the keepers. The one who gets the most stones is the winner.

## 67. Nuts in May.

THE players divide equally, and the two sets place themselves opposite to each other at a good distance apart. Those on one side take hands in a row ; those on the other do the same. The first side then advances and retires singing :—

Here we come gathering nuts in May, nuts in May, nuts in May,
Here we come gathering nuts in May, all on a fine Summer's morning.

The other side then advances and retires singing :—

Whom will you gather for nuts in May, nuts in May, nuts in May,
Whom will you gather for nuts in May, all on a fine Summer's morning?

The first side, which stood still whilst the other advanced and retired, again advances singing, and naming one of the players :—

We'll take Minnie Gray for nuts in May, nuts in May, nuts in May,
We'll take Minnie Grey for nuts in May, all on a fine Summer's morning.

The second side then asks :—

Whom will you send to take her away, to take her away, to take her away,
Whom will you send to take her away, all on a fine Summer's morning?

The first side replies :—

We'll send Mary Ward to take her away, to take her away, to take her
away,
We'll send Mary Ward to take her away, all on a fine Summer's morning.

They then spread a handkerchief, or scarf, on the ground, and the players that have been mentioned join hands and tug and tug till one is pulled over this barrier. When pulled across she goes to swell the ranks of the victorious side, and the play continues till there is no one left on one side.

## 68. Tawsey; or, Tersey; or, Tierce.

Tawsey, as played in the North of England, appears to be the same game that is called Tierce in other parts of the Country. All the company save two are placed in couples radiating from a certain centre. One of the two left out makes a third to one of the couples. The other one is a pursuer, who is to commence the game by trying to touch the outside player where there are three persons. The third person, directly he sees the pursuer making for him, slips to the inner side of a second couple and so evades being touched, as it is the outside one of three that is the object of pursuit, and whose identity, in this way, is always changing. This keeps the whole party in motion; for directly the pursued player takes up a position inside another couple, he is no longer in danger of being touched, and all the necessary precautions against the pursuit fall upon the outside one of the new three, formed by the arrival of the pursued player. It is not necessary that he should attach himself to any particular couple; all that is requisite is that he should get out of the reach of the pursuer by getting on the inner side of either of them. When the pursuer eventually succeeds in touching one of the players, he enters the circle of couples, and the person he has touched takes his part.

## 69. Baste the Bear.

ONE boy plays the part of the Bear; another that of the Bear's master. There is a rope about three yards long, which may be either attached to the bear or held in his hand, and the master must hold the other end. The other boys tie their handkerchiefs into knots and try to baste the bear with them. His master endeavours to touch them when they approach near enough for him to do so, but he must never let go the rope, nor upset the bear, who may be either crouching or sitting. When he succeeds in touching a boy, that boy becomes a bear, and is basted in his turn, and the bear becomes the master, or bear leader. The bear has the privilege of choosing his own master to begin with, generally.

## 70. Ball with Tests.

AMONG the many ways of playing with balls is one in which the players toss the ball against a high wall, and between the time the ball is thrown against the wall and caught again, various feats are performed, such as clapping the hands several times, or turning round once or twice, or touching someone else.

## 71. How many Horses has your Father got?

THIS question is generally asked of any player who is newly blindfolded. The answer always is, "Three." The next question is "What colour are they?" The answer is always "Black, White and Grey." Then the questioner adds, "Turn round three times and catch whom you may." Having turned round the three times, the blindfolded player has lost all clue to his locality, and the game (of which this is only the preliminary) begins. Blind-man's Buff is generally played in this way, and the same set of questions is asked of everyone who is blindfolded in turn.

## 72.  Here we go round the Mulberry Bush.

THIS is a game for very small children.  They must form a ring, and hand-in-hand dance round and round in a circle, singing :—

> Here we go round the mulberry bush, the mulberry bush,
>     the mulberry bush,
> Here we go round the mulberry bush, on a cold and frosty
>     morning.

When they come to the four last words "on a cold and frosty morning," they must let go of each other's hands and turn themselves completely round.  The leader then says, and performs with actions,

> This is the way we wash our hands, we wash our hands, we
>     wash our hands,
> This is the way we wash our hands, on a cold and frosty
>     morning.

When the cold and frosty morning is mentioned they all turn round, they then join hands again and go round the invisible mulberry bush as before, singing :—

> Here we go round the mulberry bush, the mulberry bush,
>     the mulberry bush,
> Here we go round the mulberry bush, on a cold and frosty
>     morning.

Whenever the cold and frosty morning is mentioned, all through, they must turn round separately.  The leader then proceeds to put them through several simple performances, such as : this is the way we brush our hair ; this is the way we black our boots ; this is the way we wash our clothes ; this is the way we iron our clothes ; this is the way we learn our lessons ; and between each representation, the ring is formed and they dance round singing :—

Here we go round the mulberry bush, the mulberry bush,
the mulberry bush,
Here we go round the mulberry bush, on a cold and frosty
morning.

The last two illustrations are generally, this is the way we go to
school, which is done to slow time ; and, this is the way we come out
school, which is sung to very quick time. All the players keep
singing the whole time, during the different movements, as well as
when going round the ring.

There is another way of playing this game for players who are
a little older. Trades are performed instead of toilet operations, and
the singers sing, between the dances round the bush, this is the way
we build our walls ; or, paint our doors ; or, make our chairs, &c., &c.

## 37.    Deaf and Dumb Motions.

THE players divide into two parties and settle which side is to begin.
The side chosen then retire to their part of the playground and
choose a trade, to imitate with "deaf and dumb motions," or complete
silence. We will say they choose to represent bakers. They come
forward and announce the first and last letter of their trade: B.R.

One of them says :—

Work is begun ! No more talk till work is done.

They proceed to pretend to knead dough, and put bread in ovens,
and open and shut the oven door to look in, and perform any other
action they think illustrates the trade, in complete silence. The

other side is entitled to give three guesses. Should they all be incorrect, the bakers retire and prepare another trade, which they announce by the initials in the same way. They repeat the same rhyme, and commence their new operations, maintaining the same strict silence. The other side may speak, till their turn comes to perform the deaf and dumb motions, when they must maintain the same strict silence and the other side may talk. Directly they make a correct guess they retire and choose a trade, and go through the same formula, giving the initials of their trade and repeating the rhyme. Those who were bakers to begin with, then have their three guesses. Should anyone speak who ought to be silent, they lose one in the counting up of the correct guesses at the end. Whoever guesses the most trades performed by their opponents is the victor. There is scope for a good deal of skill in the acting of the different trades. A dancing master, an actor, a coachman, a band conductor, a guide, and bathing attendant are suggested as affording good opportunities for the display of various accomplishments.

## 74.  The Drawbridge.

THERE should be an even number of players for this game. Two of them place themselves face to face and hold up their arms, clasping each others' hands, to form an arch, as in Oranges and Lemons. The other players in file approach and demand entrance. Those who compose the drawbridge answer: "Three times they shall pass, but at the last pass, by those under whom they pass, they will be taken." Those who are in the file pass under the bridge, the first time and the second time in good order, and repeating these words; but at the third time they make a rush to try and get through without being caught, as they are warned they will be. When two prisoners are taken they make a second drawbridge at some distance. The other players demand admittance, and the game continues until all players have become drawbridges.

## 75. The Egg and Spoon Race.

IN this race the competitors carry an egg in a spoon from one part of the playground to another. As there is a danger of dropping the egg, the pace cannot be very fast. The game is best played on grass, and the eggs should be boiled.

## 76. Jolly Welshmen.

ALL the players are against one in this game. To begin with, they keep at the far end of the playground till they all approach that one with a statement that they are Jolly Welshmen looking for a trade. Supposing there are ten of them, they say, "We are ten Jolly Welshmen looking for a trade." He asks, "What trade are you?" They reply, "Anything you like." He then says, "Show me one." They comply by acting with dumb motions the processes of some trade they have previously agreed to represent. He then guesses what they are doing, and if he should guess correctly he has to catch as many as he can before they can return to their goal. If he should not guess correctly they return, and begin over again with a fresh trade. When he has caught them all but one, he begins on his side by saying he and his companions, naming their number, are looking for a trade, and the same questions and answers are asked and given as before. Supposing they have agreed to be joiners, one would pretend to hammer, another to saw, a third to plane, a fourth to measure an imaginary piece of wood, a fifth to turn a screw, the sixth to use a brad-awl, and so on. He would probably be able to guess what they were representing immediately. If not, they can return to their goal and agree upon another trade, such as that of a baker, mason, gardener, tailor, &c. As they are caught, they must mention the diminution in their numbers, thus: "We are nine Jolly Welshmen," then "We are eight Jolly Welshmen," and so on.

## 77.　Put your right hand in.

THIS is a game for very young players.　Form a ring hand in hand. A leader then gives the word of command: "Put your right hand in," and every one must hold his or her right hand in the centre of the circle.　The leader then continues: "Put your right hand out," and every one has to put it outside the circle.　He goes on, "Shake your right hand a little and turn yourself about."　When this has been done and all have joined hands again, he goes on: "Put your left hand in," and when this is done by all, "Put your left hand out," and when this is also done, "Shake your left hand a little and turn yourselves about."　The next command is "Put your right foot in," then "Put your right foot out," and "Shake your right foot a little and turn yourself about."　The left foot is then put through the same actions.　The next movement is "Put your heads in, put your heads out, shake your heads a little and turn yourselves about." When all this is done, the leader finishes with—"Put your heels in, put your heels out, shake your heels a little and turn yourselves about." All must say the words the leader says after him, and all must re-form the circle after every turning round at the conclusion of each action.

## 78.　Lubin Loo.

LUBIN Loo is similar to the above, with the addition that the children go round and round in the ring singing :—

Here we go, Lubin Loo, here we go, Lubin Light.
Here we go, Lubin Loo, all on a New Year's night.
All your right hands in, all your right hands out,
Shake them a little, a little, and turn yourselves about.

etc., etc., etc.

## 79.　Bingo.

A RING is formed with one player in the centre who has a stick. They sing :—

There was a man who had a dog,
And Bingo was his name, oh!
B. I. N. G. O.
And Bingo was his name, oh!

G

The player in the centre then points with his stick to five players in the ring, who are to say the letters forming BINGO in the order in which he points to them. If either of them does not say the right letter he has to go into the centre, and the player who has been there joins in the ring.

## 80. Follow your Leader.

THE players all form in file behind a leader, who marches, doubles, halts, jumps, leaps, stoops, kicks, whistles, puts his hands in various positions, touches various objects, and goes through as many performances of the kind that he can manage, and all his followers have to imitate him exactly.

## 81. A Ring of Roses.

THIS game is for very little children. They form a circle, or two small circles, hand in hand, and go round singing :—

> A ring, a ring of Roses,
> A Pocket full of Posies,
> Atche-u! atche-u! atche-u!

The last word imitates a sneeze. When it is mentioned the little players all plump themselves down on the floor; or, if in an open playground, stoop down to the ground, and then scramble up again and re-form the ring, or rings, and repeat the performance.

## 82. Races with Hoops.

PLAYERS who own hoops may all stand in a row and start at once, the one whose hoop is the last to fall being the winner. One who is not a competitor must give a signal for the commencement of the race.

## 83. Races with Tops.

IN spinning tops, if several are spun at the same time a competition is set up that is sometimes very interesting.

# 84.    Poor Mary sits a-Weeping.

ALL join hands and go slowly round and round singing.    In the centre of the ring kneels one player who has her hands before her face as though weeping.    The others all sing :—

Poor Mary sits a-weeping, a-weeping, a-weeping,
Poor Mary sits a-weeping on a fine Summer's day.

They continue :—

Stand up upon your feet, your feet, your feet,
Stand up upon your feet on a fine Summer's day.

She rises, and they go on :—

Now you must choose your lover, your lover, your lover,
Now you must choose your lover on a fine Summer's day.

She makes a choice of one of the players in the ring, who comes and stands by her side, whilst the rest go on round and round slowly, singing :—

Now you must shake hands, shake hands, shake hands,
Now you must shake hands on a fine Summer's day.

They shake hands whilst they are singing this verse, and at the conclusion they kiss.    The first Mary then joins hands with the rest of the players in the circle, and the second one kneels in the centre and becomes Poor Mary.    The game proceeds till everybody has been Poor Mary.

## 85. Delving John.

THIS is a ring game with one player in the centre. All go round and round singing :—

> Delving John was dressed in black,
> Silver buttons behind his back ;
> Foot by foot, and knee by knee,
> Turn around your back to me.

As, one by one, the players are chosen by the one in the centre, they turn their backs as requested, and go round singing till all have turned their faces from the centre in this manner.

## 86. The Spanish Knight.

ALL the players but three form a semi-circle. One of the three left out is the Spanish Knight (he can have a cloak thrown over his shoulder if approved) ; another is the mother ; and the third is her daughter Jane, who must be closely veiled. The Knight advances to the mother singing :—

> Here is a Knight just come from Spain,
> To court your only daughter, Jane.

The mother replies :—

> My daughter Jane she is too young,
> She has no knowledge on her tongue ;
> Turn back, turn back, ye Spanish Knight,
> And clean your spurs till they are bright.

The Knight retreats, but immediately advances again singing :—

> My spurs are bright, and newly wrought,
> For in this country they were bought.

The mother replies :—

> Your spurs are bright ?
> Then choose the fairest in your sight.

He chooses one of the players from the circle. These two then advance, beginning again with :—

> We are two Knights come out of Spain,
> To court your only daughter, Jane.

They are refused by the mother as before, and return to ask again, when she gives them leave to take the fairest in their sight. When they have done this, all three come to the mother as three Knights out of Spain, who refuses, with excuses that are slightly varied each time.

> My daughter Jane she is too young,
> She has not learnt the Spanish tongue

and when four Knights come she says,

> My daughter Jane she is too young,
> She can't endure your flattering tongue.

When all the players, except the mother and Jane, are Knights, they all come down together, and try and steal Jane away, who is still covered up; and a little scramble ends the game. The tune sung in the north for the verses is similar to that of "Maids arise, and bake your pies on Christmas day in the morning," and "Here we go round the Mulberry Bush."

# 87.  The Sea is Agitated.

Any moderate number of boys and girls can play at this game. It requires, however, as many seats as there are players, save one. If there are no seats in a playground, and it is desired to play it, a form might be carried out for the purpose, and if there should be more players than one would accommodate, two might be used, placed back to back (proper permission having been obtained). One player, chosen by lot or counting out, or otherwise, commences the game. All the others having taken their seats, he gives each of them the name of a fish,— shark, cod, salmon, mackerel, herring, sprat, and so on. This being done, he begins to trot round and round the seats murmuring, "The sea is agitated, the sea is agitated," without ceasing. Suddenly he calls out the name of one of the fish, shark, for instance. At the call of his name, the shark must rise and run behind the conductor murmuring, likewise, "The sea is agitated, the sea is agitated," without ceasing. The conductor calls a second fish, who does the same as the preceding one, and then a third, and so on till they are all in motion, running round and round the seats and all murmuring, "The sea is agitated, the sea is agitated." At the moment when they are least expecting it, the conductor cries out, "The sea is calm," upon hearing this cry each player must cease murmuring and try to seat himself on one of the seats, it does not matter which, so that he gets one. As there is always one short there must always be a player left standing. It is he, or she, who becomes conductor in their turn, and who has to give new names to all the other players. Should there be any difficulty in thinking of a sufficient number of fish to vary the representations every time, the names of beasts and birds may be given eventually, to keep the game going ; or the same may be retained.

## 88. The String Trick.

THIS is very diverting. Grown up people are as puzzled and entertained with it as young ones. It can be performed either out-of-doors, or in-doors. You take two long pieces of string of equal length (say two yards long), and tie each end of one of them to the wrists of any member of the company willing to be coupled with another. You then tie one end of the other piece of string round the wrist of a second person, and then pass the string behind the piece tied to the first person; after which, the end of the second piece is fastened round the other wrist of the second person. They are thus tied together loosely and cross-ways, and the difficulty they have to master is to get themselves apart without untying or cutting the string. It looks an extremely simple affair. They think they have only to stoop and come up on the other side of the string to be free, and down they dip, only to find themselves still united. Then they try stepping over the strings cross-ways; this has no better effect. Then they wriggle round to get back to back. They are watched by the whole company, and directed to try various moves, and jeered and cheered on to fresh efforts time after time.

The way to get out of the entanglement is to take hold of the centre of the top string in a loop, pass it over the left hand, then under the string on the left wrist, and through this loop bring the left hand, when the two will be quite apart without untying the string.

## 89.    A Pot of Wall-flowers.

THE players join hands and form two circles. They all sing the following words :—

> Here stands a pot of wall-flowers, growing up so high;
> We are all ladies, and we shall surely die,
> Except Mary Jones, and she's the youngest girl,
> She can hop, and she can skip,
> She can turn the mangle stick,
> Fie! fie! fie! for shame!
> Turn your back to the wall again.

When they come to the third line, they choose any girl they please and put her name into it instead of that of Mary Jones. And when they come to the last line, the girl so chosen has to turn her back to the centre of the ring.

## 90. Honey Pots.

EVERY boy and girl ought to play at Honey Pots before they grow too big and heavy, for childhood can scarcely be considered complete that does not hold it in remembrance. All the players squat down with their hands tightly clasped under their knees, except two, who pretend to be buyer and seller. The first comes to the row of honey pots and asks the seller whether he can recommend his honey as good. He replies the buyer may taste it. The latter then passes from one to another of the pots, giving each a gentle tap on the head, and pretending to taste. Finally, he selects one, which they proceed to weigh, each taking hold of an arm of the honey pot, and carefully swinging it to and fro. When the hands of the honey pot can no longer sustain the strain, and they come apart, another choice is made, and fresh weighing begins, till every player has had a good swing. Every swing to and fro is counted as a pound weight. The buyer finds some too heavy, and some pots too small, by which means the game is lengthened out at will. The buyer and seller should be the strongest and tallest of the players.

## 91. Flags.

IN this game the players divide themselves into two parties, and each party takes up a position opposite the other. They then draw a line on the ground between them. They next hang their handkerchiefs in conspicuous places about the playground. Midway between the two homes of the players is a handkerchief, spread on the ground, which the players must step over before they are entitled to their flags. These are defended by one chosen for the purpose, who need not allow them to be carried off, if he can touch any of the others who try to do so. Only one flag may be captured at one time, and anyone carrying away a flag is safe from capture. If anyone is caught before they have carried off a flag, he has to remain a prisoner till one of his party comes to him, and brings him back. Which ever side gets the greatest number of flags wins the victory.

## 92.     Eagles and Children.

HALF the players are eagles, and half are children. The children form a ring, and an eagle tries to get into it by force or stratagem. When he succeeds he flies away with a child. The other eagles all do the same, until half the children are taken. Then the eagles form a ring, and the children try to get into it ; whenever they succeed they take a prisoner back with them, and proceed till they have regained them all.

## 93.     Sally Waters.

ALL the players but one form a circle, and, joining hands, dance round and round that one, who is selected to kneel in the centre of it. They sing :

> Sally, Sally Waters,
> Come sprinkle your fan,
> Here comes a young lady
> With a young man !
> Rise, Sally, rise (*the child in the centre rises.*)
> And don't look so shy,
> You will have a lover by-and-bye.
> Come ! choose from the North,
> Come ! choose from the West,—
> Choose the one you love the best.

(*Here the child in the centre chooses a partner, who enters the circle.*)

The ring of players, which stops dancing for this purpose, then resumes their movement and song :—

> Now you're married, we wish you joy,
> Father and mother shall oft come nigh ;
> Love together, like sister and brother,—
> We hope you two may kiss each other.

H

When the kiss is given, the one chosen is left in the circle, and the first player joins in it, singing the same song over again. A second choice is made when the words occur that indicate it; and when the verse is finished and the kiss is given, the second child joins the circle, and the third is left to make another choice, and so on. The words slightly vary in different parts of the country, but the drift is the same always.

## 94.        Obstacle Race.

A RACE-COURSE must be lightly traced on the ground with a stick, either oblong, circular, or straight. At intervals along its course must be placed parallel marks, sufficiently wide apart to make it tolerably difficult to jump over them. The distance between each pair of marks may be increased towards the end of the course; and the last obstacle of all may be a cord raised at a little height from the ground, by supporting it on two blocks of wood large enough to admit of stones being placed on them to keep the cord up. The cord should never be fastened, but only kept in position in the slightest fashion by a weight of some kind, so that it may give way and fall down at the least touch. The race commences at a signal given by one of the players fixed upon to be a judge. The runners all start together, and ought to be able to jump over all the obstacles without touching them or tumbling. It is, however, quite lawful to get up after a fall and continue the race. He who arrives first is the winner.

## 95.  The Cat Mewing.

ONE player is blindfolded.  The others gently move round him, or her, in a circle.  He takes hold of anyone he pleases, who immediately mews.  If he cannot guess who it is by the mew, he must let go his hold, and proceed to make another choice.  This continues till he is correct in his guess, when the player whose mew he has identified has to be blindfolded instead, and he enters the quiet circle.

## 96.  Stilts.

STILTS are easily made by nailing small cross-pieces on to sticks, and they create much amusement, first in learning to walk with them, and afterwards by making use of them.  They should not be made too high, so as to avoid any serious accidents.

## 97.  The Clothes-Basket Feat.

THERE is an amusing game to be performed with a clothes-basket and a penny, but it is best for it to be played on a grass lawn.  You put a strong stick, such as a long broom-handle, through the two handles a large clothes-basket, and support the two ends of this stick on two chairs.  The first player is then directed to get into the basket, sit down in it, and balance himself.  Some one then puts a penny on the chair behind him, and tells him to take it.  Unless extremely careful, he over-balances himself in a moment, and falls out of the basket.  For this reason the basket should only be a very few inches from the ground, to prevent any accidents.  Another player next steps into the basket, and after seating himself tries to perform the feat, till, one after another, all the company has gone through the same experience, with varied fortune.  The penny might well be considered the property of the first player who could reach it, who would, doubtless, think it well laid out if put up for competition again, till the entertainment came to an end.

## 98. Weighing.

Two players stand back to back and lock their arms in each other's, and then lift each other off their feet alternately, by bending forward in turns.

## 99. Carry my Lady a-Dandy-Chair.

Two players make a small square seat with their hands, by each clasping one of their own wrists with one hand, and one of their comrade's with the other. They then allow another player to seat herself, or himself, upon it, with her or his arms round their necks, one arm round each, for security's sake. They then carry this player about, thus seated. They sing :—

> Give me a pin to stick in my chin,
> To carry my lady a-dandy-chair.

## 100. Two in the Front.

THE players arrange themselves in couples behind each other, except one, who stands in front of the first two. This one then claps her hands three times, counting as she does so, one, two, three. As soon as she says this the last couple run round to the front, one by the left side, the other by the right side, and try to join hands at the top before the clapper catches either of them. Should one be caught, she becomes the clapper, and the other one pairs off with the former clapper immediately behind her. The new clapper then counts one, two, three, and the new last couple run up in the same fashion to the top. If neither is caught, they are simply two in the front, and the clapper has to clap again.

## 101. Rock the Cradle.

AMONG the numerous skipping games there is one called "Rock the Cradle." Two players merely sway the skipping-rope backwards and forwards for others to jump over, very slowly, with two little jumps on either side of it. In the North, this is sometimes called "Boattie."

## 102.     Pepper and Mustard.

WHEN turning the rope for others to skip over, it is customary to quicken the pace, after a time. Those in charge of the rope call out "Pepper" as they do so. After a short time they increase the speed again, with a warning call of "Mustard." When the inevitable breakdown occurs, the rope is given to the player who stops it, to turn, and the one who has been turning it joins the skippers. As there are two who turn the rope, it is the one nearest to the player who broke down that has to be relieved.

## 103.     Cross-handed Skipping.

AMONG the feats ordinarily performed with the skipping-rope is crossing of the hands, which also crosses the rope. Another is skipping double, that is, two skippers stand face to face and jump simultaneously over the same rope. This is sometimes called "Visiting."

## 104.     The Awkward Squad.

THIS is a joke as well as a game. ALL the players are drawn up in a line like soldiers, except two, one of whom is the Captain, the other Serjeant. These two have to be in each other's confidence. The Captain stands in front of the soldiers and gives the word of command. The Serjeant stands at the head of the men and obeys with the rest. A little real drill is first gone through : "Eyes front, heads up, one step forward, one step backward, one step to the right, one step to the left," and so on. Then the word is given :—"Ground right knees." This is followed by the command, "Right arms forward," and then "Left arms backward." When all are in this tottering position, the Serjeant pushes against his neighbour, who falls against the person next to him, who in turn upsets the one next to him, till the whole row is overthrown.

## 105.   The Wolf, Shepherd, and Sheep.

The player who is selected for wolf must hide himself, or retire to a distance.   The others range themselves behind the shepherd in file, holding to each others clothes, or by placing their hands on the shoulders of those in front of them.   They walk about singing :--

> Let us walk in the wood
> When the wolf is not there.

From time to time they stop and the shepherd asks, " Is the wolf there ? "   Each one answers in turn, "The wolf is dressing ; " or, "the wolf is putting on his boots ; " or, "the wolf is getting on his hat," &c.   After each answer, walking and singing re-commences. At last, when this has gone on for some time the wolf cries out in answer to the question, "Yes, the wolf is there," and makes a rush at them, and tries to seize a sheep.   They all shelter themselves behind the shepherd, who cannot be taken, and who keeps the wolf away as long as he can.   When a sheep gets seized he becomes a wolf.   Sometimes it is settled beforehand that the same player must remain wolf till he has seized a certain number of the sheep.   But it is always the first sheep who is taken that has to be wolf.

## 106.                    Pies.

A game is played in America in which there are three principal performers, as well as the rest of the party, who are children.   One is a nurse, one a mother, and the other a baker.   The mother leaves all the children in charge of the nurse and goes away.   Directly she is out of sight, the baker makes his appearance and asks for a match to light his fire with.   Whilst the nurse looks for a match, he steals one of the children and carries him or her away to his home or shop. He then returns and asks again for a match, and when the nurse turns her head runs off with another child. The third time she refuses, upon which the baker resorts to stratagem, and tells her the kettle is boiling over. When she retires to attend to the kettle another child is stolen; and in this manner, one after the other, all the children are carried off by the baker. He makes them into pies by standing them all in a row, with their hands over their faces. Their mother enters the shop to buy a pie to take home to them. She enquires of the baker what kind of pies he has. He replies mince, apple, gooseberry, and so on, lengthening out the list to correspond with the number of children. The mother taps one on the head and pretends to taste. She exclaims, "Why this tastes like our Polly! Polly!" The child says, "Yes, mother." The mother asks, "What brought you here?" The child replies, "My great toe." "Then run away home," says the mother, and she does so. Another child is then tasted, and the mother continues, "Why this tastes like my Jenny," and the same dialogue is carried on, and the child sent home. The third child tastes like her Sally, and after as many questions is sent home. Till, at last, they are all recovered by the mother.

## 107.     Hunt the Ring.

THE players form a circle, leaving one in the centre of it. A long piece of string, with a curtain-ring threaded on it, is tied in a circle of about the same size as that made by the players. They all take hold of it, and pass the ring about from one to another. It is the business of the player in the centre to guess who has the ring. His task is made as difficult as possible, by all sorts of false movements on the part of those who are hiding it with their hands. When he guesses correctly in which hand the ring is concealed, he joins the circle, and the player he has detected with it takes his place.

## 108.    Hunt the Slipper.

HUNT the slipper is somewhat similar, only the players are seated in a circle on the ground, and the guesser walks round and round outside it.    He brings a slipper to the cobbler to be mended and asks when he shall return for it.    He goes away whilst the others hide the slipper under themselves.    When he returns for it they declare it is not ready, and a fresh appointment is made for him to come again. After another disappointment or two, he is told he must hunt for it, and he then tries to find it by searching every likely member of the party, that he thinks is hiding it.    Whilst thus engaged, the slipper is passed to another part of the circle and rapped on the ground to show where it is ; and as he runs round to it, it is again passed round under the players' knees.    When he gets possession of the slipper, he joins the circle, and another brings it to be mended over again.

## 109.    Soldiers.

PLAYING at soldiers has always been a favourite amusement of the playground.    The Captain should tell his men to form a line, and stand at "attention," heels together, body straight, head erect, shoulders thrown back, hands hanging easily at the sides.    He should then number them, one, two, all along the line.    His first word of command after this is done, is for the twos to step forward.    This brings his forces into two rows, one slightly in front of the other. They can now go through a few simple extension movements.    There are several evolutions that can be gone through, such as marching, halting, forming a square, right wheeling, left wheeling, marking time, forming fours, saluting, &c.

When marching in a single file, at the young captain's order "Form double file," every alternate soldier takes one step to the right and one step forward.    They are then in double file.    When the captain says "Form fours," the two second men all down the double file take a step to the right, and then one to the front; they are then in fours. When the captain says " Wheel to the right," the right-hand man, or pivot man, must mark time, while the next to him takes small steps towards the right, and the next to him longer steps, and at the same time the outside man is taking the larger curve that is required. When the captain says " Wheel to the left," the pivot man, who is the one on the left-hand side, marks time, and the next to him takes short steps, the third longer, and the fourth longest of all. In marking time, first one foot, then the other, must be raised about three inches from the ground without advancing; this is continued till the order Forward, Quick March, or Slow March, or Halt, when the movement ceases with precision.

# 110. A few Simple Extension Movements.

CLOSE the fists as if holding dumb-bells. At the word " One," raise the arms above the head; " Two," bring the hands down to the shoulders; " Three," stretch the arms straight out sideways; "Four," double the arms so that elbows are on a level with waist, and fists touch the shoulders; " Five," hands straight down at the sides; " Six," bent up back again to shoulders; " Seven," stretched straight out in front level with chest; " Eight," drawn back to shoulder; afterwards resume attitude of attention.

A second movement is as follows: "One," raise arms above head, and interlock the thumbs; " Two," lower the arms with thumbs locked, bend body down and touch toes; " Three," raise arms above head again; " Four," arms to fall at sides, as at attention.

A third movement: " One," hands on hips and heels closed; "Two," lunge forward with right foot, at the same time raising right arm; " Three," resume position of hands on hips and heels together; " Four," lunge forward with left foot, at the same time raising left arm.

I

To salute: At the word "One," each little soldier must bring his right hand with a circular motion to his head, palm in the front, with the point of the forefinger one inch above the right eye, thumb close to the forefinger. At the word "Two," let the arm fall to the side This is gone through again with the left hand.

## 111.        The Birthday Present.

A LEADER goes round a circle of players, and beginning with the first one asks: "What did you have for a birthday present?" Supposing the answer is "a watch," the enquirer goes on to ask every odd question he can think of, and to them all, the same answerer must reply "a watch" without laughing. Thus he might ask, "What have you got in your mouth?" Answer: "A watch." "What would you like to have for dinner?" Answer: "A watch." "What will you wear to-morrow on your head?" Answer: "A watch." "What shall I give the dog to eat?" Answer: "A watch." He must go on asking these random questions till the answerer is obliged to laugh; or, it may be settled beforehand, that there shall be only a certain number of questions asked before passing on to the next player, should he have been able to keep his countenance up to that time.

## 112.        Pig's Feet.

THIS is a similar game to the last mentioned, with the difference that the answer given to every question must always be "Pig's Feet." Supposing you turn to one of the players and ask, "What is your name?" The answer must be given seriously, "Pig's Feet;" or, you may ask, "What have you got in your purse?" The same serious answer must be made: "Pig's Feet." The constant reply, at last, elicits a burst of laughter. When this comes, the player who put the questions enters the circle, and the one who first laughed has to be the questioner.

## 113.                Les Graces.

THIS game is played with two, four, six, or eight players. Each is furnished with two long light sticks. These sticks, or canes, are for the purpose of discharging a small light hoop towards the opposite player, who must catch it on his, or her, own sticks. It is very similar to Battledore and Shuttlecock. The points of the two sticks crossed hold the hoop in the air for a moment, and then a dexterous movement of uncrossing them sets it flying towards the opposite side. It must be caught before falling to the ground, on the point of the stick of the partner. Each pair of players are opposed to the others, and which ever pair keeps the hoop from falling for the greatest number of passes are the victors. Proficients sometimes use two hoops, which cross each other in their transit to and fro, and are both caught, one by each of the two opposite players.

## 114.    Battledore and Shuttlecock.

IN this game two players oppose the rest, tossing the Shuttlecock to and fro with the Battledore. Or it may be played singly, the aim being to toss up the Shuttlecock and receive it on the Battledore as many times as possible. To make the game more intricate, four may play corner-ways, or cross-ways; or six, or eight may play in any order agreed upon. Always the highest score is the winner.

## 115.    Here is a Poor Widow from Sandiland.

A BIG girl, or grown-up person, is the Widow, and the rest of the players are all her children, except one more big girl or grown-up person. The widow begins to advance with all the children hand-in-hand, singing: " Here comes a poor widow from Sandiland, with all her children in her hand, one can bake, and one can brew, and the other can make a lily-white doo ; please will you have one of my daughters?" (or sons, either, as the case may be). The second grown-up person, or elder player, takes one. This is all gone through over and over again till the children are all transferred to this second woman, who then becomes the widow.

## 116.  King of the Castle.

A PLAYER stands on any little elevation that he may find, and asserts that he is the King of the Castle. His play-fellows try to pull him down, and he on his part tries to maintain his position. The old provocative doggerel ran :—

> I am the King of the Castle ;
> You are a dirty rascal.

Should a play-fellow displace his King, he becomes his successor.

## 117.  Winding up the Clock.

ALL take hold of each others' clothing, as in hen and chickens, following one behind the other. They run round and round in a series of diminishing circles, until they are wound up into a close knot round the leader, all the time saying tick, tick, tick, tick. Then they reverse, unwinding the clock, until they are in a long straight line as before.

## 118.  Balloon Tennis.

BALLOON Tennis is played with large wooden spoons and a half-penny balloon, or inflated bladder. The object of the game is to keep the balloon in the air, by tossing it upwards with the spoons.

## 119.  Blindfolded Aim.

FASTEN a small piece of paper on to a wall or door ; or make a small chalk mark that can be seen at a short distance. Then blindfold one of the players, and tell him to walk up to it and touch it. He is pretty sure to touch a spot at a considerable distance from it, although he may think he is walking in a straight line to it. The rest of the company are then blindfolded, one after the other, and requested to walk up to the same mark and touch it. The one whose aim is the best, or goes nearest the tiny target, is the victor. A piece of paper the size of a postage stamp is sufficient.

# INDOOR GAMES.

———◆———

## "I am sure we should all be as happy as kings."

# INDOOR GAMES.

## 120. The Family Coach.

EVERY player takes the name of some part of the Family Coach, or of its horses or occupants. For instance, one is Mr. Demi-semiquaver the owner, another is Mrs. Demi-semiquaver, a third is Master Demi-semiquaver, and a fourth the beautiful Miss Demi-semiquaver. The rest are the coachman, footman, near horse, off horse, wheels, doors, harness, till every one has a part. Someone then begins to tell how this Demi-semiquaver family received an invitation to spend Christmas with a relative at some distance, and how the coach broke down as it went along, what happened to the different members of the party, how the near horse behaved, what the off-horse did, what damage was done to the coach and harness, and how the footman had to go on foot for assistance. This narrative can be lengthened and embellished at the pleasure of the narrator, and all sorts of amusing incidents introduced into it. The point in the play is that as often as any parts of the coach and its belongings are mentioned, the person representing either of them has to get up and turn round, and when either of the family is mentioned, the player representing that person has to get up and turn round, and whenever the Family Coach is mentioned in its entirety, the whole company has to get up and turn round. Sometimes a forfeit is the penalty for obliviousness or non-performance of the turning round, and sometimes a nudge is given by the nearest neighbour to delinquents, according to the age and taste of the players. This is an old game of never failing interest. If there should be more players than there are articles already suggested for representation, more can be invented by mention of the items packed in a Christmas hamper that was on the top of the coach, and of the costume worn by the beautiful Miss Demi-semiquaver.

## 121. Clumps.

THE players in the room are divided into two clumps, or groups. One representative from each clump leaves the room; these two, when outside, agree upon some subject, person, or thing, that is to be guessed by those inside the room. They then return to the room, and one goes into the centre of one clump, and the other into the centre of the other clump. The clumps are really opposition camps, and those in the one try to find out before those in the other can do so what it is that has been thought of by the two representatives Each of these last is rapidly surrounded by questioners, who, in whispers, so as not to be heard by the opposite clumps, put such queries to them as " Is it a town ? Is it a person ? Is it alive ?" and so on. Whichever clump guesses correctly first gains possession of the two representatives to augment its members. Two others are then chosen, one from each clump, who retire and choose a subject as before. The aim is for one clump to absorb all the players by virtue of their correct guesses and consequent capture of the two who have been out.

## 122. Extemporary Lectures.

ALL the players who are clever and old enough to play at this game must write upon small scraps of paper the name of some subject they consider suitable for an Extemporary Lecture. Each folds his, or her, paper neatly up, so that the word written upon it cannot be seen, and each puts the tiny billet into a hat. When all are seated, the first player must rise and take out of the hat one of the billets.

He must then place himself where he can conveniently face all the rest, in front of the fire-place, on the hearthrug, for instance ; and for three minutes or more (as may be agreed), he must lecture upon the subject that he finds mentioned in the billet, when he unfolds it Some of the fun depends upon the subjects chosen ; but more upon the methods of lecturers ; and perhaps, even more, upon the discomfiture of those who are unable to think of anything to say. We will suppose the first subject picked out of the hat is playfellows. The lecturer might say something like this: "Playfellows are of various kinds: some are delightful, and some are more so. Some are young, and some are less so. Most of them have one characteristic in common, which is a great facility for passing away time pleasantly. There are but a few of them for whom you could not better spare better folks ;" and so on, till his time is up, when he must re-seat himself with the rest. The next player then dips his hand in the hat, and takes his place on the rug, or rostrum, and unfolds his subject. We will say it is riches. He might begin his discourse on them in some such fashion as this :—" Riches have been described as a snare ; that is not my experience of them. They have never ensnared me, nor made any efforts to do so. My own opinion of them is that they are indescribable, and unfathomable. A pocket full of marbles would be riches to some people. A pocket full of rye has been mentioned as a possession of price ; and a pocket full of gold would be dire poverty to others, especially on pay days. Riches are relative, like a nice cousin ; and strange, like night-mares ; as well as common-place, like contentment." Story books, toffee, lessons, games, people in general and particular persons, are a few more suggestions. The succession of lectures should be kept up till all the players have lectured.

## 123.  Your Left-hand Neighbour.

ALL the players seat themselves about the room, or in a circle. One goes out, to whom the game is new. It is then explained to all in the room that he will return, and will be told they have all thought of the same thing, and he is to guess what it is. They are told also that what they have thought of must be their left-hand neighbour. Whatever question may be asked, each has to reply with reference to their left-hand neighbour. As the left-hand neighbour of one may be a girl, and of the next a boy, the answers are so bewildering that it is next to impossible to form any idea of what has been thought of. We will suppose the player outside has been called in. He might say, "Is the person thought of fair or dark?" The answer would be made according to the complexion of the left-hand neighbour of the person who has been asked the question. The question to the next player might be, "Male or Female?" to which the reply would be made according to the sex of the left-hand neighbour of this person. Going on to other players in rotation, answers might be elicited that quite contradict these two statements, such as the dark person of one description might have yellow hair in another, owing to the change in the personage of the left-hand neighbour; and a person under ten by one account, might be over twenty by another. But it must always be a person who does not know the game that is chosen to go out of the room and then come in and guess what has been thought about.

## 124.  Odd Readings.

THE company seat themselves, and each member of it chooses a trade, except one who is going to do the reading. When the preliminaries are settled, the reader takes up any story book, or magazine that may be handy, and begins to read. In the course of the reading, he abruptly stops and looks at one of the company, who must immediately call out a word relating to his trade. The more out-of-the-way the word is to the subject matter of the reading, the more laughter is evoked. We will say the reading is an account of a wedding. It would be something like this :—"The bride was

attired in a white —" here the reader looks to the member of the
company who has chosen to be a miller, who calls out "sack of flour,"
and the reader goes on " richly wrought with," and then looks to a
joiner who calls out " shavings ; " going on again he adds, " she
carried in her hand a beautiful —" here the reader looks at the iron-
monger, who shouts "frying-pan," "and was attended by six—" here
he turns to the florist of the party who calls " bull rushes." He
continues, " on the conclusion of the ceremony the happy pair and
large company were entertained by the bride's mother to—" here he
might turn to the confectioner who might say "sugar plums." He
resumes, "The presents were—" and turns to the grocer who calls
out " figs and prunes," or any other article he chooses to name out
of a grocer's shop ; and goes on, "It is understood the honey-moon
will be spent in—" and if he should turn to a musical instrument
maker, the reply might be " a violin." The account would thus
read, " The bride was attired in a white sack of flour, richly wrought
with shavings. She carried in her hand a beautiful frying-pan, and
was attended by six bull-rushes. On the conclusion of the ceremony
the happy pair and large company were entertained by the bride's
mother to sugar-plums. The presents were figs and prunes. It is
understood the honey-moon will be spent in a violin." Of course
the readings must never be twice alike.

## 125. The Sculpture Gallery.

ALL the players go out of the room, but two. One of these then
poses as a statue, with or without the assistance of any drapery that
may be at hand. When the representation is settled, and the attitude
assumed, the other calls in a player from the outside, and addressing
him, or her, confidentially, says something to this effect, always
varying the words according to circumstances : " Now, can you
make any suggestion by which this statue can be improved ; any
difference in the attitude ; or any extra arrangements anywhere ? "

The player thus confidingly addressed generally ventures on some recommendation; or, if he should not, spontaneously, is artfully induced to do so eventually, and directly the words come out of his lips, he is requested to assume the exact attitude he means, and to remain in it by the side of the other statue. A second person from outside the room is then called in, who finds two statues before him, he is asked to recommend any improvement to them that he can think of, and when he falls into the trap and ventures to make a suggestion, he is pounced upon to carry it out himself, and a third person from outside is called in. He finds three statues in the gallery, and on his opinion being asked as to the position of their limbs, or the carriage of their heads, or the expressions of their countenances, is pretty sure to be induced to make some remarks, when he is likewise required to assume the manner he recommends, and thus a fourth statue is created. Another player is called in and victimized in a similar manner, and then another, till all have become statues, and the gallery is complete. There is scope for great diversity of treatment of the statues, and for skill in eliciting the various suggestions from the players. The amusement at every fresh addition to the gallery, made in this unwonted manner, is great.

## 126. The General Post.

EVERY player must be seated save one. And each player must choose a country for a name. The player who has no seat announces that the general postman has brought a letter from one country to another, and those who represent those places must exchange seats directly, and as they are doing so, the player without one must try and slip into one or the other. Should he succeed, the player whose seat he has obtained must then be the general postman. We will say that one player is France, another Italy, a third Greece, a fourth Russia, a fifth China, a sixth Japan, and so on. The general postman cries out " Here is a letter from China to Japan," and away run the two players who represent those two powers to exchange seats, and whilst they are doing so he will make a rush to get into the one he thinks he is the most likely to reach. We will say that he secures the seat of Japan. The player left unseated then announces, in like manner, that he has brought a letter fro n another place to another, say France to Italy, and the same scramble occurs again. Should he not be nimble enough to secure one of t! e vacant places, he has to remain postman, and name two other countries. Until he succeeds in getting a seat he has to go on naming two countries in this same manner.

## 127. A Snap-dragon.

A SNAP-DRAGON is made by placing a lot of raisins in a dish, and pouring over and around them some brandy, gin or whiskey. This is placed in the centre of the table, and all the company present assemble round it. A lighted piece of paper is then applied to it, when it bursts into lurid flames. The fun consists in snapping out the raisins with finger and thumb. When they all have been got out of the flames, the next step is to sprinkle a handful of salt into the spirit, which then takes on very peculiar colours, and imparts to the faces of those around the most supernatural effects. Every time the fire seems to be going out, a vigorous shake of the dish will make it give out fresh flames.

## 128. Can you do this, this, this?

LIFTING up a spoon, or similar article, with the left hand, you pass it into your right hand, and give three taps on the table with it, asking your neighbour at the same time, "Can you do this, this, this?" You will find your neighbour will, generally, take the spoon with his right hand, and give three taps whilst he asks the same question. Of course, you tell him that is not the right way, and he tries again, or passes it on to his next neighbour.  When all the company round the table try, and fail, you point out to them that they did not begin with the left hand before using the right one.

## 129.  The Hissing Game.

ONE player retires outside the door, whilst the rest agree which of the company he shall sit beside, when called in.  When this is settled he is told to enter, and he tries to seat himself by the side of the player he thinks likely to have been selected for him.  If he should make a correct guess, this person goes out in turn; but if he should make an incorrect guess, all the company hiss as loud'y as they can, and he has to go out again.  When a boy is sent outside the room, a girl is generally chosen as the person by whom he is to seat himself.  When it is a girl who is sent out, a boy should be selected for her to seat herself by.

## 130.  One-and-Twenty Questions.

ONLY one-and-twenty questions must be asked in this variation of the game of questions.  The questioner has to leave the room and begin his labours over again, after a new object has been selected for him to ascertain, if he should not be able to make a correct guess after asking one-and-twenty questions.  These questions, at first, have to be leading ones, and carefully condensed, so as not to waste any of them.  Thus the questioner should ask whether it belongs to the animal, mineral, or vegetable kingdom, which would bring him a reply that would limit the range of his wonderment materially.  Supposing the largest Elephant in the Zoological Gardens is fixed upon.  The answer in this case would be "animal."  The questioner, therefore, need think of nothing but animal life, except articles manufactured from it.  So his next question should be, "alive or dead?"  The answer to this gives him the information that it is a live animal.  "Where is it?" brings him the reply that it is in the "Zoo."  The answer to "large or small?" brings him very close to a certainty, and he can either ask a few more questions, as he is far from the full number of twenty-one, or hazard a guess. He may make only three guesses. Should none be right, he has to be told what it is, and made to leave the room whilst another object is selected, and then begin again.

## 131. Buzz.

FOR this game the players may either stand, or be seated, at their pleasure. It consists of counting, with the peculiarity that every time the figure seven is come to, or any form or combination, or possible division, the word Buzz must be substituted for it. When anyone makes a mistake by mentioning seven, or seventeen, or twenty-seven, or any of the higher amounts made by multiplying seven, they have to retire from the contest. A leader begins by saying one, the next person says two, the next three, the next four, the next five, the next six, the next Buzz; the rest go on rapidly counting one more each till they come to thirteen, when the next player has to say Buzz; and then they go on again till they come to sixteen, when the next player has to say Buzz. Instead of twenty-one, Buzz must be said; again instead of twenty-seven and twenty-eight, Buzz must be said. By degrees, through inattention, the number of counters gets reduced till there are but two left, and then these two go on alternately till a slip leaves one of them the victor.

## 132. Fizz, Buzz.

IN Fizz, Buzz, all the fives and sevens are missed in counting, and the word Fizz substituted for all fives, and multiples of five, and the word Buzz uttered instead of seven, or any combination of it, as in the Buzz game. This is a little more intricate than plain Buzz. A very large party can join in this game, and every mistake is attended by instant dismissal from the circle.

## 133.  Musical Chairs.

A ROW of chairs, one facing one way, the next the other way, the third the same way as the first, and so on alternately, is placed in the centre of the room.  There must be as many chairs as there are players, save one.  A merry tune must then be played on the piano, or some other instrument, whilst every one in the company dances round the chairs.  The musician suddenly ceases in an unexpected part of the tune, when all must try and seat themselves.  As there is a chair short, there will always be one left without a seat.  The music goes on again, and the dance round the chairs is resumed.  In placing the chairs, alternately facing one way and then the other, there is a little extra difficulty created.  It is usual to remove a chair every time the music ceases, and for the person left without a seat, to be left out of the dance each time.  When the dancers are reduced to two, and the chairs to one, and it is a question which of the two will get possession of the remaining seat, the rest of the company are still interested in the game.

## 134. My Aunt has come Home from Paris.

A DOZEN players, more or less, can play at this game seated in a circle, or semi-circle.  The first player remarks that his, or her, Aunt has come home from Paris.  The next person enquires, " What did she bring you ?"  The first player replies, " A pair of scissors," with a motion of the fingers of the right hand like scissors cutting, which motion has to be kept up till the end of the game.  The second person then turns to the third, and repeats the statement, " My Aunt has come home from Paris."  The third player then asks, " What did she bring you ?"  The second declares it was a pair of scissors, and commences to make the same motion with the fingers of the right hand that the first player is making.  This remark and reply, with the continuous motion of the right hand fingers goes on all round the circle, or semi-circle. When all the company are performing this motion, the first player begins again with the remark that his Aunt has come home from Paris. The second player asks, as before, "What did she bring you?" The reply is "a fan," and with the left hand spread out fan fashion, a movement imitating that of a fan is kept up, as well as the scissors movement made with the right. After this second statement, question, and reply have all gone round, the first player, for the third time, announces that his Aunt has come home from Paris, and in reply to the second player's question, "What did she bring you?" says it was "a snuff-box," and gives a loud sneeze, the other two motions being kept up simultaneously. When this has gone the round, and the whole party is sneezing, and fanning, and moving their right hand fingers as though cutting, the first player announces again that his Aunt has come home from Paris, and in reply to the second player's enquiry as to what she brought him, says "a spinning-wheel," and begins to work an invisible one with his right foot. When this has gone the round, and they are working their right hands and right feet in the ways described, the same routine is commenced once more, and to the question of the second player, "What did she bring you?" the answer is "a sewing machine," with a corresponding motion of the left foot. After this, the oft repeated statement of the return, and the enquiry what the Aunt has brought, elicites the fact that it is "a cuckoo clock." This adds the constant cry of cuckoo! cuckoo! to the commotion. One more round of "My Aunt has come home from Paris," and "What did she bring you?" adds a Poll Parrot to the collection of gifts. Besides the actions of the hands and feet, the sneezing, and the call of the cuckoo, there is now the addition of the words "Pretty Poll, Pretty Poll," to the bewildering and laughing commotion, When this addition has gone all through the circle, the game is over, and the players will be glad of a few minutes' rest.

L.

## 135. Shadow Plays.

THE⁻E are actions performed behind an ordinary sheet, hung up, and stretched. There must be an extra strong light behind the performers, to make good shadows. The audience, who must be seated in front of the sheet, do not require a light. The performers act any little by-play they can arrange, such as a boy helping himself to jam from a high shelf, and being caught in the act ; or, a wrestling match ; or, a dancing lesson, in dumb-show.

## 136. Turning the Trencher.

WHEN the company is seated, a player turns, or spins, a trencher or circular tray, and calls out the name of another of the players. The one thus called, however, is not to move, but his right-hand neighbour is to run and catch it before it falls. If the owner of the name should get up by mistake, he has to pay a forfeit, and if his next neighbour should fail to catch the trencher before it falls, he has likewise to pay a forfeit, all of which are cried and redeemed at the conclusion of the game.

## 137. Thumbs Up.

THE company should be seated round a table for this game, with their thumbs round the edge of it, and informed by a leader that when he mentions that "Simon Peter said Thumbs up," they are to put their thumbs down, and when he says " Simon Peter said thumbs down," they are all to put their thumbs up. Each player keeps both hands close to the table, and follows out these instructions with both. The fun consists in the confusion of ideas arising out of the rapid way the leader repeats his order, or formula, some of the company generally fai ing to put their thumbs up and down at the right times, which are the reverse of those that are called out. As each one makes a mistake he leaves off playing, till, at last, there is only one player left, when it is interesting to see how long he can keep on without confusing the commands. The leader is at liberty to repeat either of his orders consecutively now and then, to make the remembrance of their reverse nature more puzzling.

## 138.　　A Comical Concert.

THE players sit round the room, each pretending to play an instrument agreed upon, each performer choosing a different one. There is a conductor, who keeps time, and who suddenly stops the performance, and asks one of the performers why he is not playing more accurately, or some similar question. The reply has to be given instantaneously, and must agree with the nature and capabilities of the supposititious instrument. Thus, should the conductor pounce upon the drummer with the enquiry "what is the matter with your drum?" he must give an answer that would really apply to a drum being out of order, such as the parchment has given way, or the cords have come loose. He must not give the same answer twice, consequently it becomes a little difficult to invent a fresh misfortune for the drum, when the drummer is pounced upon several times. It is the same with the other musical instruments. The ingenuity of the company is taxed to find new disorders for them, after they say their mouth-pieces are lost, or come loose, or their strings snapped, or bridges broken, or pegs dropped, as the case may be. If the player is unable to find an excuse, he must leave the band.

## 139.　　Hunt the Thimble.

THIS is not the same as the thimble game. The players have to be seated in a circle, with their hands in their laps, except one, who commences the game by entering this circle, and hiding the thimble, after many feints, in the closed hands of one of the other players. It is somewhat on the same lines as Hunt the Slipper, only no indication is made as to the whereabouts of the thimble, nor is it passed about like the slipper. When, after pretending he has given the thimble first to one, and then the other, it is placed in one of the circle of closed hands, the other players take it in turn to guess where it is. If neatly hidden, its whereabouts can be rarely guessed without many mistakes. No one has two guesses. The one who is correct, takes it and hides it again, in the same way.

## 140. Peter Works with One Hammer.

THIS is a game for very young players. They must be seated. A leader says "Peter works with one hammer," and raises one hand, and pretends to hammer with it. All the rest of the players do the same. The leader continues, "Peter works with two hammers," and raises the other hand, and pretends to hammer with that also. All the other players do the same. He goes on, "Peter works with three hammers," and hammers away with one leg, as well as with his two hands. The rest do the same. Then he says "Peter works with four hammers," and the other leg is brought into the same motion, the rest all performing the same movement as well. Then he continues, "Peter works with five hammers," and he nods his head; and finally, he states, "Peter works with six hammers," and he begins to rise and sit down on his seat, continuously, all the rest doing the same, and keeping up all the other motions at the same time. In addition to the motions, the other players must all keep repeating his words, and change them every time he changes them, from hammer to hammers. At the close of each movement, the word "cease" indicates when it is to be discontinued. "Peter works with one hammer, one hammer, one hammer, one hammer; cease!" All must cease instantaneously, or pay a forfeit, or retire.

## 141.        Neighbour Codfish.

ALL the players are named after fishes, and each one must remember, not only his, or her own name, but that of his, or her neighbour.

# 85

One might be salmon, another herring, a third haddock, others sole, mackerel, pike, lobster, &c. When this is settled, the following conversation goes all round the circle, and whoever forgets his name, or that of his neighbour, must pay a forfeit. Directly the players ask, or are asked a question, they must wriggle about like fish in water. The forfeits are cried afterwards.

> *First Player.*— "Neighbour Codfish, how art thee?"
> *Second Player.*—"As you see, sir, as you see!"
> *First Player.*— "How is Neighbour Salmon next to thee?"
> *Second Player.*—"I'll go see, sir, I'll go see."

The second player then turns to the third, wriggling, and asks:

> *Second Player.*—"Neighbour Salmon, how art thee?"
> *Third Player.*— "As you see, sir, as you see!"
> *Second Player.*—"How is Neighbour Herring next to thee?"
> *Third Player.*— "I'll go see, sir, I'll go see."

The third player turns to the fourth:

> *Third Player.*— "Neighbour Herring, how art thee?"
> *Fourth Player.*—"As you see, sir, as you see!"
> *Third Player.*— "How is Neighbour Haddock next to thee?"
> *Fourth Player.*—"I'll go see, sir, I'll go see."

The fourth then turns to the fifth, wriggling, like all the rest:

> *Fourth Player.*—"Neighbour Haddock, how art thee?"
> *Fifth Player.*— "As you see, sir, as you see!"
> *Fourth Player.*—"How is Neighbour Sole next to thee?"
> *Fifth Player.*— "I'll go see, sir, I'll go see."

In this way the fun goes all round the circle, and the crying of the forfeits brings it to an end

# 142. Wax-works.

WAX-WORKS are a never failing source of amusement. Each player must "dress up," to represent any character he, or she, pleases. When ready, they are told to take up a position at one end of the room, as in an exhibition or show. One of the party acts as showman ; another as musician. If there are a few members of the party left, to perform the part of the audience, so much the better. When everything is settled, and the musician seated at the piano, or provided with some other instrument, the showman must pass round the group of pretended wax figures, and with some loud-sounding rattle, pretend to wind them up. They must all stand as motionless as statues till the music begins, when they must all at once begin to make curious slow and jerky movements, till the music stops. We will say one player represents Little Bo-peep. She must keep slowly turning her head from one side to the other, as though looking for her sheep. Another, representing Old Mother Hubbard, might slowly lift her arm, as though opening an imaginary cupboard. A little Boy Blue might slowly and stiffly blow a horn. Little Red Riding Hood, with her basket on her arm might mark time with her feet, as though going through the wood. Little Miss Muffit might pretend to be frightened at a spider, that she could draw towards her by means of an invisible and elastic thread. The Queen of Hearts might make some slow motion with her hands as though making tarts. A King might count money ; a Queen eat honey ; a Maid hang out clothes. A King lifting a cover up and down off a black-bird pie, makes another good subject. Jack Horner, Tom, the Piper's Son, and all the characters in other nursery songs are also available. Historical personages may be simulated by the more advanced performers. Directly the music stops, the figures must become motionless again. If a curtain can be contrived to roll up and down, or drawn aside, in front of the collection, the success of the entertainment is increased.

# 143.    The Letter Games.

THERE are various games to be played with letters, mounted on cardboard, or written on small squares of paper.  One very simple one is for a leader to give each of the other pla. c s some particular letters, the same to each, for them to make out what they spell, and to see which can make it out first.    Thus, the letters O.D.N.U. puzzle many players for a long time, till someone sharper than the rest, finds out they spell UNDO.  Some words lend themselves exceedingly well to this game.  Few people, for instance, would guess for some time that A.C.E.R.U.S. re-arranged spells  AUCER.  And if told to make "ONE WORD" out of "NEW DOOR," are quite mystified till they find that the re-arrangement of the same letters spells both of the couples of words.    In the last century it was a fashionable amusement.  A letter, dated 1770, mentions nine letters, E.E.E.W.Y.A.I.L.K. with which the fashionable world was amusing itself to get six words, all correctly spelt.    And Miss Austin makes use of the letters forming the word Blunder in a scene in one of her stories, where this game is being carried on.

# 144.    The Gaberlunzie-man.

IN the merry game of the Gaberlunzie-man, everyone taking part in it is assigned an imaginary musical instrument, which he must pretend to play.  One has an invisible fife, another a cornet, another a trombone, another a violin, and others a guitar, flute, piano, harp, cymbals, tambourine, &c., &c.  The Gaberlunzie-man has a drum. All join in singing the following words, each pretending to play the instrument that has been assigned to him, or her, including the Gaberlunzie-man, who is the leader :—

Oh ! the Gaberlunzie-man, oh ! the Gaberlunzie-man,

We will do whate'er we can to follow the Gaberlunzie-man.

Suddenly the Gaberlunzie-man leaves off pretending to play the drum, and begins to play some other imaginary instrument, say for instance, the violin, when the player who has hitherto been playing it, must cease doing so, and begin to play as on a drum. Directly the Gaberlunzie-man begins the drum movement again, the violinist has to cease drumming and return to his fiddling; or, supposing the Gaberlunzie-man leaves off drumming, and commences to play an invisible guitar, the guitarist has to cease twanging, and begin drumming instantaneously, and with equal celerity has to resume guitar playing the very moment the Gaberlunzie-man begins to drum again. Every lapse of watchfulness that results in a mistake or non-observance of these rules, has to be paid for with a forfeit. These are cried afterwards.

# 145.    Something in the Room.

THIS is a simple game.   No one leaves his or her seat.   The person chosen to begin says, "Something in the room beginning with A," or B, or anything according to the article chosen.   For instance, if the first player should fix his mind on the fender for the rest to guess, he will say, "Something in the room beginning with F;" and the rest will look round, and ponder till they have found something in the room.   But if they have guessed something else beginning with F, that is not the fender, they have to go on guessing, and perhaps some one will make the correct guess after all.   The one who is right has then to think of something, and says, supposing it is the rug,

"Something in the room beginning with R," and then the rest all try to be the first to guess it. The initial letter being given makes the task an easy one.

## 146.     Tip it; or, Up Jenkins.

THIS is a somewhat similar game to Hunt the Thimble, only the players must be seated round a table ; the thimble is passed under the table and hidden in one of the hands of one of them. A small party is the best for it, consisting of about eight or a dozen persons, and it must be divided into two sets, one of which plays against the other, from different sides of the table. Before commencing, the players must settle how many successful games shall constitute the victory. Suppose twelve are agreed to. One side then commences. All hands of that set are placed under the table, and the thimble secretly deposited in one. At a signal, which is sometimes "Up Jenkins," they are then displayed tightly closed on the table, with the knuckles uppermost. The opposite side then begins to guess which hand holds it. This is done in this way :— The first player points to any hand that he thinks has not got the thimble concealed in it, and says "Take that away," and goes on ordering each to be taken away, till there are only two left, when he must guess which of the two has it. If he should guess correctly it counts one to his side, and he takes the thimble, and the opposite side have to guess who has it, when he has passed it under the table to one on his own side, in the same way. If he should be incorrect, and the thimble is in any of the hands he has ordered to be taken away, then the same side retains the thimble, and scores one. In the continuance of the game, the players guess the whereabouts of the thimble in rotation, in the order in which they are seated, till it is found, when the same process is gone through on the other side. Whichever side makes up twelve correct guesses first, wins the victory.

M

# 147. Mrs. MacKenzie's Supper-Party.

THIS is an amusing game, intended to be played by one or two confederates, for the surprise and entertainment of those who have not taken part in it before. Each member of the company is called out of the room, one by one, to receive an invitation. The leader of the fun is outside the door, and tells each one, privately, that when a plum pudding is mentioned as part of the supper provided by Mrs. MacKenzie, he, or she, has to run out the room as quickly as possible. Each person returns to the room, and expects that a different dish has been named to everyone, instead of the same to all. When each one has received this intimation, which is called an invitation, and they are all once more comfortably seated in the room, the leader comes in, and begins a rambling narrative to the effect that once upon a time Mrs. MacKenzie gave a grand supper-party. She did her very best to make the affair as splendid as possible, with music and flowers, and spared no pains to make the banquet as delicious and delightful as she could. And then an enumeration of the dishes she provided is entered upon, according to fancy. A boiled turkey, roast beef, pigeon pie, tongues and chickens, may be mentioned. As the narrator goes on, each member is on the tip-toe of expectation that the dish will be named that is to set him, or her, running out of the room. When, at last, plum pudding is mentioned, there is a general rush to the doorway, in which the company, if large enough, often gets completely blocked. If the narrator takes pains to describe the good lady's party in an interesting manner, adapted to the age of the company, this makes an entertaining incident in an evening's amusement.

# 148. Portraits.

THIS game is conducted on the same lines as Consequences and Reviews of Books, with slips of paper that have to be folded down and passed on from neighbour to neighbour, for additions, at the different stages of its progress. When seated at a table, and each provided with a slip of paper and a pencil, the game is commenced with an order from a leader for every player to draw a head at the top of their slips. This done, the papers have to be folded down, so that the heads are hidden, and each passed on to the next player. The second order is to draw a neck. When the necks are folded down and passed on, each to the next neighbour, they are ordered to draw a body on each slip, and when this is folded down and passed on, legs are called for, then feet. Lastly, the name of some one is to be added. When unfolded and passed round, much amusement is afforded, as there are often birds' or beasts' heads on the bodies of other creatures, and still more wonderful combinations with human features and limbs. And the name representing the supposed original of the portrait, adds to the entertaining jumble of ideas.

## 149.    Shadow Portraits.

A GOOD deal of amusement is to be found in making Shadow Portraits. These are not shadows of rabbits, cats, dogs, fish, &c., cast on the wall by different arrangements of the hands, with which children are entertained in nurseries, but portraits of people present at the time. You pin up on the wall a sheet of paper sufficiently large for a life-sized portrait. Then place your subject close against it, and with a long pencil passed down the profile of his face, you mark an outline of his features on the paper. These outlines are often so astonishing that there is a strong desire expressed to be "done" once more, and thus a pleasant hour is spent. An exhibition of the portraits side by side, on their completion, adds to the interest of the proceedings.

# 150. Pigeons Fly.

PIGEONS Fly is somewhat similar to Thumbs Up and Thumbs Down. All are seated round a table with their hands on it, and the leader calls out "Pigeons Fly," and imitates the motion of wings with his hands. All the players do the same, and then return to their quiet position. He then calls out that other birds fly, naming them one by one, according to his fancy, and always imitating the motion of flying as he does so. All the players follow his lead. He suddenly calls out the name of something that does not fly, such as "Pigs Fly," when, if any of the players thoughtlessly make a motion as of flying, they must pay a forfeit.

# 151. Proverbs.

THE original way of playing proverbs was for one player to retire from the room, whilst the rest settled which proverb they would choose for him to guess. When settled upon, a word out of the particular proverb chosen was given to each player, which word he was to introduce into his reply to any question that the guesser might put to him. We will say the players make choice of "When things come to the worst they must mend," and call the guesser in. His first question might be "How are you to-night?" The answerer might say "Quite well, thank you; when I feel ill I will mention it." His next question might be "Are you going to stay late to-night?" and the answerer must bring in the word "things," such as "No! I am thinking of putting on my things as soon as this game is over." Supposing the guesser says coaxingly to the next player, "You might give me some clue," the reply might be "Come now, that is too cool." "Where shall you go for your holidays?" might be the next query. Then "to" must be brought in, and then "the" after that, and "worst" in the next reply to that, and so on; but most probably before the guesser will have asked as many questions as have brought him so far along, he will be able to guess which proverb it is. If not, he must ask another question in which the word "they" must be introduced ; and then "must" should be included in the reply, and finally, "mend." The player whose word has enabled the guesser to come to the right conclusion is the one to go out of the room and take a turn at the guessing.

## 152. Crambo.

In Crambo, one of the players leaves the room whilst the others fix upon a word that he is to guess. When this word is decided upon, he is called in, and told of another one that rhymes with it. He then proceeds to ask questions so as to find out what it is. The other players have all to introduce into their answers a final word that also rhymes with the one chosen. We will say, for example, that Twine is the word chosen, and Line the word mentioned to the guesser on his return to the room. He begins his questions, perhaps, by asking the first player, "Do you feel the cold this evening ?" The answerer might say "Oh ! no, it is too fine." Then passing on to the next player he might ask "Have you to go home early to-day ?" and the answer might be "No, not till nine." "Have you had some tea ?" he might ask the next, who might reply, "No, but I have had some wine." Then, "Are you sorry Miss Ward is not here ?" might elicit the reply "No, I never pine." "Is this your handkerchief ?" "No, it is not mine." The last person who gives an answer before a correct guess is made has to leave the room the next time, and be the guesser.

## 153. The Figure Game.

A long evening indoors may often be spent pleasantly by means of the Figure Game. Each player has four sets of figures from one to sixteen (simply marked on little squares of cardboard, about half the size of a postage stamp). They are spread out in neat regular order before each player, with their faces uppermost. The conductor has the same amount of figures before him, higgledy-piggledy, with their faces downwards. He takes up one, looks at it to ascertain the number on it, and calls it out, and the other players have to take a corresponding number out of their own quantities, and begin to form a column with it. The aim in view is to get four rows of the numbers in consecutive succession, beginning with one and going on to sixteen, notwithstanding that they are called for at random. Those who manage to do this first win the game. We will suppose a 16 is turned up first. As this is of no use for the beginning of a line it is placed aside. Should the next be 14, this is of no present use either, and should be placed aside adjoining the 16. When another 16, or any high number is called, it must be set aside also, always keeping the highest numbers at the head of the column, and the lower ones below them, so that when the time comes to use them, they may not be blocked or inaccessible. Only six columns of these inopportune numbers are permitted. We will say 1 now turns up. With this the player begins to form one of the real columns of the game in another place. The next may not be a 2, consequently any other number must be put in the columns of inopportune numbers mentioned. Perhaps there may come another 1 directly. With this the player begins his second row. Having now two rows in course of formation, he is able to use more of the figures that turn up, without having to add them to the inopportune columns. And when the full number of four is established, the task becomes easier still. The game becomes difficult, and sometimes impossible of achievement, when the numbers come in an adverse manner that will not lend itself to any methodical adjustment of them. As a rule, however, it is possible to get the four lines arranged consecutively, notwithstanding that the numbers are taken out of a heap with their faces unseen, promiscuously. Attention must be given to the desirability of always looking to the columns of what have been termed the inopportune numbers, so as to introduce any that may be available from that store into the real rows in course of formation.

There is a limit to this use, because it is only the bottom figure in either of the six columns that may be taken to place in either of the four rows that are being formed. The diagrams show the four rows in course of formation, and the reserve columns. The pile from which the numbers are taken promiscuously must be understood as being also on the table. It will be seen if 8 were called next, the 8 in the fourth column could be put in the second row, when the 9 above it could be put next to it, and then the 10 above that can be put in position. The 11 in the fifth row could then be brought down. When a 6 is called there is one in the second column that could be brought down to the third row, and so on.

| 16 | 14 | 15 | 16 | 15 | 14 |
|----|----|----|----|----|----|
| 10 | 9 | 12 | 10 | 14 | 11 |
| 9 | 7 | 11 | 9 | 11 | 10 |
| 8 | 6 | 9 | 8 | | |
| 6 | | | | | |
| 5 | | | | | |

| 1 | 2 | 3 | 4 | 5 | 6 | 7 | 8 | 9 | 10 | 11 | 12 | 13 | 14 | 15 | 16 |
|---|---|---|---|---|---|---|---|---|----|----|----|----|----|----|----|
| 1 | 2 | 3 | 4 | 5 | 6 | 7 | | | | | | | | | |
| 1 | 2 | 3 | 4 | 5 | | | | | | | | | | | |
| 1 | 2 | | | | | | | | | | | | | | |

This figure game is on the same principle as the game of cards known as Patience.

## 154.    Beasts, Birds, and Fishes.

THE players must be seated, except the one who is to commence the game, for whom there should be no seat. He suddenly turns to one of the others telling him to name either a Beast, Bird, or Fish, whichever he selects, before he can count six. This is the prescribed form in which the demand must be made: "Beast of the field, one, two, three, four, five, six;" or, "Bird of the air, one, two, three, four, five, six;" or, "Fish in the sea, one, two, three, four, five, six." If unable to name the creature indicated before the counting is over, the player thus discomfited has to give up his seat to the questioner, and then has to ask one of the other players to name either of the three kinds of creatures in the same way. The suddenness with which the question should be asked very frequently has the effect of confusing the player, who is questioned to such an extent that he will name a fish when asked for a bird, or a beast when asked for a fish. These mistakes lead to a great deal of laughter. Suppose you suddenly turn to the player farthest from you and say, "Beast of the field, one, two, three four, five, six; " in the hurry to speak before the counting is over he will often cry out ostrich, or whale, or something else instead of the name of a quadruped. He then loses his seat, and has to demand of someone else, in the same peremptory fashion, the name of one of the three kinds of creatures. We will say he turns sharply to the person next to him and says, "Fish of the sea, one, two, three, four, five, six." It may happen that the player so suddenly accosted will call out in his confusion, "cow," when he will be seated again, and the "cow" guesser will take his place.

## 155.   Proverbs told by the Piano.

THIS is a good game, but it requires a piano. The player who is to guess the proverb that the piano will indicate must leave the room, and in his absence a particularly well-known proverb is agreed upon, to be played by the rest of the company. He and the person at the piano must be confederates, and both must understand the following mode of procedure, which must be carried out carefully, and unknown to the rest of the company. We will say the company fix upon the good North-country statement, that "Many a mickle makes a muckle." The person conducting the game then seats himself at the piano, and his confederate is called into the room. The pianist then strikes a chord for each letter in the alphabet till he comes to M, when he stops, as though he had made a mistake ; and after playing a solitary note, which the confederate will know means the vowel A, he begins again and runs fluently up to N. Stopping short once more, he re-commences and goes on, chord after chord, until he has struck twenty-five, indicating the letter Y. The guesser now knows it is a proverb beginning with "Many" that he must think of. The pianist goes on, after a solitary and hesitating note for "A," to spell "Mickle," letter by letter, with chords and notes in like manner, and the guesser is able to come to the conclusion that "Many a mickle makes a muckle" is the proverb agreed upon. If the piano is managed with skill and ease, it will be a long time before the general company make out the method by which the pianist conveyed the necessary information. Another "try" is generally asked for, and another after that. To give a second illustration : "A faint heart never won fair lady," may be chosen. After one note, as though uncertain how to begin, but which the confederate will know means A, the player strikes six chords, thereby intimating the letter F, then one note for A, then three for I, then fourteen chords for N, and twenty for T. This will spell "Faint." By the time the player has spelled out "Heart," the guesser will know that "A faint heart never won fair lady" is the proverb selected. It is seldom that a guesser is so far "abroad" as to require the whole of the proverb to be laboriously spelled through. In conducting the game it is well to choose a saying that is a familiar one, so that it may be easily recognised. It will be seen that consonants are represented by chords, and the vowels by single notes.

# 156.    The Railway Dance.

PARTNERS for this game are chosen in the ordinary way as for other dances. There must be a Musician and a Master of the Ceremonies. When the Musician is ready, the M.C. calls out "take your places for the lancers," and the dancers lead out their partners. The Musician plays (on a comb should there be no better instrument), and the players all dance. As soon as they are fairly started the M.C. calls out "a polka," when the tune is instantly altered without stopping, and the dancers begin to polka. They have scarcely got into full swing when the M.C. calls out "a quadrille," and the music, without stopping,

N

changes again, and the dancers have to commence a quadrille.
Directly this is arranged and in course of prompt execution, a waltz,
or gallop, or saraband, or country dance of some kind, is demanded
by the M.C., and as soon as these are commenced a fresh change is
made to lancers, or minuet, or some different dance.   These constantly
repeated changes make a great deal of merriment.   The M.C. may
call for what he likes, and may repeat his command for any particular
dance as often as he likes.   The game calls for a little skill on the
part of the musician to accompany all the changes instantaneously,
but in the general scramble no very great notice is taken of the
music.   It is necessary to begin with a square dance,

## 157.          Thought Reading.

THE players form a ring, except one, who goes out of the room, and
is the thought reader.   A confederate is necessary, who acts as
medium.   The company fix on a number, and the guesser is called
in from the outside and asked to state what number has been thought
of.   He joins the circle, taking care to place himself by the side of
the medium, who quietly and secretly presses his hand with distinct
movements, according to the number decided on.   If six has been
chosen, he gives six distinct pressures, and the thought reader
announces confidently that six is the number that has been fixed
upon.

## 158.     The Four-legged Puzzle.

ANOTHER kind of sham thought reading in guessing things that have
been thought of by the rest of the party, whilst the diviner is out of
the room, has been invented for merry-making purposes.   When the
guesser comes into the room, his accomplice always names an article
with four legs immediately preceding the question to which it is
necessary he should answer in the affirmative.   This four-legged
article should be different every time, so as not to give a clue.   Thus

he may ask, "Is it this book? Is it that picture? Is it that ink-stand, or the poker, or that chair, or this ornament?" and his confederate will say " Yes " to the last question, because it follows mention of the four-legged chair. In the same way, after " Is it a horse?" he would answer " Yes " to the next question.

## 159. Magic Identification.

Two confederates announce that one of them will leave the room whilst the rest of the party settle among themselves which one of the others he shall name when he is called in, which he will do without asking a single question, or looking to the right or the left. Before leaving the room, however, he requires that every one should sit per-fectly still; and when all are motionless, he lingers about till one of the party accidentally makes any slight movement. Then, making sure, by a glance, that his confederate has also observed the same accidental movement of that particular person, he leaves the room. Now it is necessary, for the success of the identification, that the confederate in the room contrives that the person selected for him to point out should be the one who has slightly moved. This part of the business is conducted in whispers, and is easily and quickly managed, any other suggestion being cleverly over-ruled without exciting suspicion. Then the confederate outside is called in, and he walks straight up to the player who made the slight move-ment before he left the room. As he does not even look at his accomplice, it is a great wonder to all that he is so certain and so prompt. The secret of his performance is rarely guessed. It adds to the general amusement to let some others try, who, of course, all fail to identify the person chosen.

## 160. Poker Writing.

POKER Writing may be done with a walking stick quite as well as with a poker, should there not be one that is available. In this game there are two principal performers, who are to a certain extent confederates, in so far as they must both understand the plan of the peculiar writing. The rest of the company choose a word, which is to be written by one of these performers and guessed by the other. Whilst the company is deciding upon the word, the player who has to guess it must leave the room. It is a good plan for the company to be told merely to point to any object in the room for it, so as to be sure the guesser cannot overhear it. We will say they agree to fix on the word "picture." The guesser is then called in by his (or her) confederate in the room with a sentence beginning with the first letter in "picture," such as "Pretty politeness on our part to keep you out so long," or, "Pray come in." After a few flourishes with the poker, which mean nothing, though they must be made elaborately on the ground as though writing, the writer gives three taps on the floor with it, each tap representing a vowel in their right order. So far the guesser knows that P and I are the two first letters. The writer must then bring in some remark, naturally, that begins with C, such as "Careless people are not particular how they spell every word in this sort of writing, but I am." And after some more waves, as though still writing, he may go on to a sentence beginning with T, such as "There, now, I am sure you will guess the word in a minute." Five more sharp taps, introduced among the flourishes, will then indicate the letter U. "Really you must be tired of standing," brings in the letter R, and the writer has only to give two light taps for the letter E, when the whole word is spelled out. Long before getting to the end, probably, the guesser will have been able to make up his mind what the word is. He makes his guess, and so saves his colleague further trouble. The company is generally very much puzzled as to how he comes by his information. Often one player will feel confident that he too can guess any word the rest may choose, and triumphantly leaves the room so that they may decide what it shall be. He is, of course, unable to do so when he tries. The two confederates then repeat their performance.

All the one in the room has to remember is to begin sentence after sentence with the consonants of the word chosen, and to give light raps to represent the vowels: one rap for A, two for E, three for I, four for O, and five for U, as they come; and all the guesser has to do is to keep his wits about him, so as not to miss any of the first letters in any sentence spoken by his colleague, no matter to whom it is addressed, nor any of the raps as they occur in the grand flourishes made on the floor. To give another example, we will say a " chair " has been selected. "Come in" will do for the first letter; a hesitating look at the floor, and then " How shall I begin? " will do for the second; a few graceful flourishes and a tap, a few more flourishes and three taps, and then " Really, this is too simple," and a laugh, finishes it. The guesser has noticed the C in " Come in," the H in " How shall I begin," the one rap for A, the three for I, and the R in " Really," and confidently guesses " chair." The writer must be very particular to make no remark whatever, except those necessary for the indication of the consonants.

## 161.      Musical Fright.

THIS is played to music on a piano. There is a row of chairs, which has one seat too few for the players. When the performer begins to play a merry tune on the piano, the players take hands and dance round the chairs in a ring till he suddenly stops, perhaps in the middle of a bar, and they have to seat themselves. The one left out is now out of the game, and one chair is removed. The performer on the piano begins again, and when all the other players are dancing round the remaining chairs, stops as suddenly as before. The one who is unable to get a seat retires, and a second chair is removed. This diminishing process is carried on till there are only two players left to dance round one chair. The one who obtains the seat is the winner of the game. It will be seen there is scarcely any difference between this game and that of Musical Chairs. The chairs need not be placed alternately, as in the last-mentioned ; and the hand-in-hand ring, formed for the Fright, differs slightly from the single file that runs round the chairs. Both forms of the game are general favourites.

## 162. The Brush Puzzle.

You take a clothes brush, and ask another player to stand up with his back to you. You then ask him to count how many times you brush him. You begin by gently brushing his back with the brush, but after a few strokes you brush yourself with it instead, and merely stroke him with your hand. He cannot tell the difference, and nearly always guesses the full number of times he has been touched as having been brushed. Of course you must make the stroke of the brush and that of your hand as much alike as possible. You then go on to test the perceptions of other players, one after another, the rest looking on. Anyone guessing correctly how many times he has been actually brushed may take the brush, and call upon anyone else to be brushed, who, in turn, guesses how many times he has been really touched with the brush.

## 163. The Rule of Contrary.

This is an amusing old game for very little players. All hold a hand-kerchief, or, if there are many players, a tablecloth, by the edges. An elder in charge then says, "Now this is the rule of contrary, when I say hold fast, let go; and when I say let go, hold fast." "Hold fast!" They ought then to let go, but some are sure to hold fast by mistake, when they must pay a forfeit. The leader then begins again with the same statement, always trying to come in unexpectedly with her command to "Hold fast" or "Let go," and all those who make mistakes must pay forfeits. These are cried afterwards.

# 164.     The Shouting Proverb.

ONE player goes outside the room.   In his, or her, absence a proverb
is chosen and a word out of it given to everyone present.   The outside player is then called in, and someone appointed to do so having
counted three,—One, Two, Three,—all, simultaneously, shout the word
that has been given to them.   He, or she, has to guess what the
proverb is that is thus instantaneously and noisily told to them.
Supposing the proverb chosen is "A stitch in time saves nine," as
there are only six words, if there are more than six players two of
them must have the same word.   The effect is very odd, something
like a terrific sneeze.   A sharp ear, however, is generally able to
distinguish a word or two that gives a clue to what it is.   The
player from outside must continue guessing till correct, the others
repeating the shout occasionally to assist him.

# 165.     Thought Reading Séance.

A CONFEDERATE is necessary for a Séance of this kind.   One is
easily instructed how to proceed.   It is best to instruct one before
the game is announced as about to begin, because then no attention
is drawn to the subject till all is ready.   You must tell your confederate, or partner in the fun, that when you want him, or her, to point
to the first book or article that you will ask the company to think
about you will make use of one word in calling him, or her, into the
room.   If you want him to point to the second you will call him in
with two words.   If he is to point to the third, you will use three
words ; if the fourth, four words, and so on.   When you have quite
explained this, you may remark to the general company that thought
reading is a very curious art, and if agreeable to them you will show
them how it is done.   You will request your confederate to leave the
room whilst the company selects something in it that they will think
about.   When this request has been complied with, take five or six,

or more, books, or little ornaments, and place them in a row, and ask them which they will think about. Supposing they choose the one nearest to the door by which your confederate will enter, you will call out one word, such as "ready." When he comes in he will walk straight up to the first book, or ornament, and point to it. Supposing they choose the second you will call your confederate in with two words, such as "come in," and he will point to the second article. Supposing they choose the third, you must use three, such as "we are ready," and he will point to the third; if it should be the fourth, four, "now then, come in;" and so on. These little phrases must be constantly varied to throw the company off the scent. Another time the one word might be "enter;" the two, "ready now;" the three, "we are waiting;" the four, "quite ready, at last;" or, "come in, my dear;" the five, "come in, we are settled;" and six, "you must be tired, come in." If the same words should be repeated every time, the clue to the mystery will be too easily found. You must puzzle the company as much as you can by requesting them all to keep their thoughts on the article they have chosen, and not to let them wander. And you must fully explain to your confederate to begin to count the articles from the end nearest the entrance, because if he began to count from the wrong end the reading would not come right. He may pretend to be drawn to the article against his will by the force of their thoughts.

## 166.    Sixpenny Telegrams.

ONE person gives out twelve letters from the alphabet. The rest of the players have each to compose a sensible telegram, the words of which are to begin with the letters mentioned, and in the same order as that in which they are given. The first and last letters are to be used for the names of the persons to whom each telegram is addressed and from whom it is sent. When they are all finished, they are read aloud.

## 167.  The Ring and String Game.

MAKE a circle of string on which is strung a ring. The players all stand in a circle holding this string and trying to hide the ring with their hands, as they pass it from one to another on the string. One player stands in the centre of the circle, and makes a grab at the hand he thinks covers the ring. If unsuccessful he must try again till he succeeds, and the player in whose hand he eventually finds it takes his place, and goes on with the game.

## 168.  Yes or No.

YES or No is a similar game to questions, with the difference that all the replies to the questions must be given with either of the two words, Yes or No. One player goes out of the room while the rest fix on some object (it does not matter where it is,) that is well-known, such as Cleopatra's Needle, the gold ball on the top of St. Paul's, Dick Whittington's stone on Highgate Hill, the Lord Mayor's state carriage, Big Ben, the Monument, the New Tower Bridge, or the Marble Arch. When the selection is made, the outside player is called in and asks the others, in rotation, any questions he thinks will enable him to form ideas that will ultimately lead him to a correct guess. He must begin with the one seated nearest to him on his entrance, and take them one after the other, and then begin again, if he should not have arrived at a solution of the mystery when he comes to the last. As everyone has heard of London Bridge, we will suppose that is the object that has been chosen. The enquirer might ask, "Is it alive?" The reply would be "No." Then, "Does it belong to the mineral kingdom?" The reply would be "Yes." "Is it public property?" The answer would be "Yes." Then the questioner might go on, "Is it in a street?" The reply would be "No." Then, "Is it in London?" "Is it on land?" "Is it a fixture?" "Is it in a retired spot?" "Have I ever seen it?"

The enquirer would here run over in his mind all the facts he has elicited,— that the object is public property, belongs to the mineral kingdom, is not on land yet is a fixture, and is not in a retired spot. He will think it must be a bridge, and with another few questions will guess the right one. The person who has answered the last question is the one who must go out next.

## 169.   Questions.

IN this game you may fix on what you please in the absence of the person who has to guess what it is, and make what answers you like to his questions, providing they are not misleading. It is surprising how very soon a correct guess can be made, notwithstanding that the object selected may be quite an out-of-the-way one, such as the Lord Mayor's chain; or, the wedding ring of the Lady Mayoress. Supposing we fix upon a lamp-post in front of the Bank of England, it might be identified with only a few questions :— "Where is it?" "What is it made of?" "How large is it ?" "Is it moveable ?" would give us the facts that it is in front of the Bank of England, is made of glass and iron, is about eight feet high, and immovable. It would be difficult to think of anything else but a lamp-post that would correspond with these particulars.

## 170.   Towns.

EACH player must have a pencil and a piece of paper. A leader mentions a letter and a time, say three minutes, and the players write down as many towns beginning with that letter as they can remember in three minutes. We will say the leader calls out F, and four minutes. The players write down all the towns they can think of, the names of which begin with F. When the four minutes are up, those who have the most get a mark. The leader gives out another letter and another limit of time, and the rest go to work again. Whoever has the most marks in the end is the conqueror.

## 171. Mrs. Mackias is dead.

THE players arrange themselves in a ring, and are seated. The leader begins by saying to the person next to her, or him, "Mrs. Mackias is dead." She asks, "How did she die?" The leader replies, "With one finger up," putting her finger up as she says so, and keeping it up till the conclusion of the game. The player she addressed repeats the same piece of news to the person sitting next to her, who makes the same query and receives the same reply, as do, in rotation, all the others. The leader then begins again, with the statement that "Mrs. Mackias is dead;" and in reply to the question, "How did she die?" reports that it was with one finger up and a blind eye. When this has gone round the ring, and all are sitting with one finger up and one eye closed, she repeats the same news; and in reply to "How did she die?" declares it was with her mouth all awry, upon which all the players draw their mouths down. The game can be kept up as long as different causes for the demise can be illustrated.

## 172. A Surprise Party.

A SMALL plate of raisins is required for this game, or a paper tray may be made that will hold as many raisins as there are players. Everyone leaves the room except the leader, who is the host or hostess of the Surprise Party, and who calls in first one and then another, separately, till all are in the room. When the first is called in, supposing it is a girl, she is told to sit by the leader, or hostess, or host, as the case may be, and open her mouth wide. At the sight of the raisins she naturally expects that one of them will be put into her open mouth. But it is not so. That is the surprise. The leader tells her to open her mouth wider still, and then quietly puts the raisin into her own mouth and eats it herself. The next member of the party is then called in and told to seat herself, or himself, in the same friendly way, and to open her, or his, mouth wide ; and while this second mouth is wide open, the leader proceeds to eat the second raisin. A third member of the party is next called or invited in, and told to sit down and open his, or her, mouth, and the leader calmly eats the raisin as before, those in the room enjoying the surprise, disappointment, and fun exceedingly. This goes on till all are in the room, and the leader has eaten all the raisins.

## 173.  The Immovable Squad.

THIS is one of the games that can only be played successfully with novices. The player who acts as drill-master, and understands the fun to come, ranges his men against a wall, and makes every man's right shoulder and right foot touch it firmly. After impressing them with the fact that they are not to remove this contact with the wall, he gives the word of command, " Left foot forward," when it will be found they are all unable to move and must remain in this position, unless they are allowed to come away from the wall.

## 174.  A Tea-party Trick.

You inquire of the company if they can do this :—You wave your first finger in a circle on the table, saying, " A round thing ; " then in this circle you indicate two smaller circles, and say, " two eyes ; "

then make a stroke for a nose and say, "a nose," and a crossway one for a mouth, saying, " and a mouth." All this you do with your left hand. The next person to you tries to do the same, marking with their finger on the cloth, " a round thing, two eyes, a nose, and a mouth," successively. But he is sure not to have noticed that you used your left hand instead of your right. Whereupon you gravely say, "No, it is not quite right." Then the next person tries, and of course with his right hand. Probably several will try before any one suspects that it is only a matter as to which hand is used.

## 175. The Tuft on the Table.

A SMALL tuft of cotton wool is placed on a polished table, and the players stand round and blow it, without allowing it to fall from the table. Should they blow it off, they must pay a forfeit.

## 176. The Electric Battery.

THIS is a game that must be played by confederates for the surprise and amusement of one person at a time, who has not seen or heard of it before. A few small empty jam pots, or bottles, say four or five, are required, and round each one a piece of wire must be tied, leaving one end long enough to be held in the hand. This is to give the idea of an electric battery to the person who is to be electrified. These slight preparations should be made privately. When the time arrives for the game to begin, all those of the party who have not joined in it before, and consequently do not know it, must leave the room. In their absence, those who are going to conduct the game must produce the jam pots, or small phials, on a tray, and settle among themselves which particular pot, or bottle, they will pretend shall be the source of the electric current. One person at a time is then admitted, and told to hold the little collection of wire ends from each pot in one hand, and with a finger of the other hand to touch first one pot and then the other. When he touches the particular pot previously agreed upon before his admittance, all the company in the room scream as suddenly and with as much noise as they can, which makes the victim think for the moment, that he has been electrified. When the laughing is over, the next person is admitted into the room, and the same performance gone through again. The wires are placed in his hand, as in the first instance, and he is told to touch every pot very carefully, with any other mystifying instructions that may occur to the operators at the time, such as the necessity of being cautious on account of the force of the electric current. When he touches the pot agreed upon, the same loud and instantaneous scream is to be set up. When all have been admitted, and all, one by one, joined in the scream attending the electrifying of the rest of the party, the game is at an end.

## 177.  Telephone.

Two performers, who are confederates, mystify the rest of the players in this game. The rest are seated round the room, and are told to sit still and be as quiet as possible, because of the requirements of the telephone. The two confederates take a long stick, and one places one end to his ear and the other places the other end to his ear. They pretend to listen attentively. Then one announces that the other will leave the room, and whilst he is out they will fix upon one of their number in whose hands they will hide a coin, and on his return he will be able to mention which it is, by virtue of the telephone. The two confederates quite understand that the one about to leave the room, must know before he does so, which is to be the person selected. To arrange this, they again pretend to listen to the telephone, asking the company to be perfectly quiet and still. They listen, or pretend to do so, till one of the company moves accidently. This one is to be the person selected. He then declares he heard something through the telephone, and leaves the room. The minute he has gone, the remaining confederate arranges that the person who has unconsciously moved, is to be the one who is to have the coin, and when it is given to him to hold in his hand, or put in his pocket, he calls in his friend, who walks up to the person who has moved, and says, "This is the one mentioned as having the coin by the telephone." As it is more fun to keep the secret than to let all the audience know how it is done, the same players repeat the game with the choice of a new person with whom to deposit the coin, till the audience tires of it ; unless it should be the same person who is the one to move again, when he would be chosen once more.

# 178. Bouts Rimés.

THIS is a pastime for players with bright and sharp wits. They sit in a circle, and the leader either composes a line of poetry or reads one out of a book, and the player whom he picks out has to make a second line to rhyme with it with sense and rhythm, or pay a forfeit. Often the leader spins a top and the second line of the couplet has to be made up before it ceases to gyrate, or the forfeit has to be paid Example:—"As years pass on, a change time makes." This might be capped with "'tis well 'tis so, for all our sakes ; " or, "Bring in the holly from the snow," might be capped with "Don't forget the misletoe ; " or, "Great Cæsar sent out a decree," to which reply might be made "I'm sure it was not meant for me." The more fun put into the capping the better. "Through the blind, the sun streams wide upon the floor," might suggest such a cap as "Better to have entered by the open door."

# 179. Pit-a-Pat.

Pit-a-pat, pit-a-pat, baker's man !
So I do, sir, as fast as I can.
Pit it, and pat it, and mark it with T,
And put it in the oven for Tommy and me.

THIS is a game to play with very little folks. One hand is put on the table, then one of the child who is to be amused is placed on that ; on the top of these two hands is placed the second hand of the amuser, and on the top of all, the other hand of the child. Whilst repeating the rhyme the lowest hand is withdrawn, time after time, in rotation, and placed on the top of all, till the fun interests the child no longer. Other children can join in.

## 180. Hot Cockles.

HOT COCKLES is the name of a game in which one of the players hides her face in the lap of a lady, who places her hand on the back of the kneeling figure. One by one the other players approach and give the open palm a slap. The kneeling player has to guess who it is that has given the slap. Sometimes she is not able to do so for some time. When she does guess correctly, the giver of the particular slap she has identified has to kneel in her place.

## 181. Mock Tiddley-wink.

WHEN seated round a table, it is easy to improvise a rough and ready "Tiddle-wink" by placing any receptacle that is at hand, such as the lid of a small box, or a saucer, or a tray, on the centre of it as a pool, and then taking any buttons, counters, nuts, or other small articles that may be accessible and aiming them in turns into it. Those who succeed in tossing, or jerking their button, or counter, or nut into the pool, are to have two turns in succession. The one who gets all his pieces in first is the winner, just as in the real Tiddley-wink with a proper cup-like centre and counters of two proper sizes.

## 182. Tableaux Vivants.

TABLEAUX VIVANTS are an endless source of amusement. They are just as amusing when got up without preparation as when elaborately rehearsed, though, perhaps not so elegant. The gloom that a wet afternoon has brought into a community of youngsters bent on some outdoor relaxation may be effectually dispersed by their means. Newspaper masks, newspapers made into semblances of high-peeked head-dresses, or cocked hats; old shawls, and a few articles of such easy acquirement as canes, or sticks, are sufficient accessories with which to concoct costumes at a moment's notice. We will suggest the subject of Cinderella's Sisters dressing for the ball. One girl may be standing, whilst Cinderella is in the act of arranging a shawl as a train, and another holding a newspaper bouquet ready for her use; or, the Prince may be kneeling before Cinderella with a paper slipper for her to try on; or, Fatima, decked in a paper turban, may be staring at the stain on the key; or, a Redcross Knight might represent "Blow, warder, blow," with a paper trumpet, &c. The chief difficulty is the necessity of a curtain to rise and fall upon the groups. One rough and ready way to get over this is for the arrangement of the figures to be made close to a door outside the room occupied by the rest of the party, that is, by the necessary audience. When ready, an acting manager can open the door, when the doorway will make a kind of frame to the living picture. Suitable music made by singing through thin paper over a comb, is a pleasing addition to the proceedings, and might occupy several of the audience. When carried out on a grander scale, such as when a curtain of a large bay-window is available, the potentialities become much more extensive. Historical scenes may then be attempted, and a larger number of figures introduced.

## 183. The Foot Trick.

You announce to the other players that you will allow any of them to write on a piece of paper any word they please, in whatever language they choose, and then fold it up and stand upon it, and you will tell them what is on it. Someone will probably take up the challenge, and write some out-of-the-way word down. You tell him to fold it so that it cannot possibly be read. When this is done, you ask him to place it on the floor and stand upon it. You must pretend to consider a minute, and then say something to this effect: "Now, I said I would tell you what is on that piece of paper, and I will keep my promise. Your foot is on it."

P

# 184.    A Toy Symphony.

GIVE every player a toy instrument, and should there not be sufficient toys that make a noise, a bunch of keys, a rattle, the poker and tongs, and similar articles may be used to eke out the required number. When everyone is thus provided, down to the youngest and up to the eldest, they should be seated like an orchestra, or round the room.    The conductor then must play a lively march or well-known tune on the piano, if there is one; if not, a makeshift must be made with something else, such as a Jew's harp, or a banjo.    When the tune is played the first time, all this band of toys and implements of noise join in, keeping good time, which must be well accentuated. The second time the first part is played only one toy is to accompany it for say eight bars, as a solo, and then the whole band joins in once more.    A second toy then takes a solo of the same length, followed by the whole band again; a third follows, then the band again; a fourth, then the band; a fifth, then the band once more; and so on till every performer has played a solo to the accompaniment of the leader's instrument.    Let us suppose, as an example, that the tune "Tom, Tom, the Piper's Son" is the tune chosen. The band, consisting of every available toy, tambourine, whistle, castanets, dogs that bark, birds that chirp, drum, fife, penny trumpets, and any other article out of which sound can be obtained, begins with the leader and keeps time with him to the end.    He then repeats the tune for eight bars (not to be too long), whilst the tambourine only accompanies him.    The band joins in for the next eight bars; then the whistle only continues with the accompaniment for eight bars, after which the band joins in again.    Then the next solo is performed by a little barking dog, or piping bird, or mewing cat, and there is generally a burst of enthusiasm when the band comes in once more.    The different amount of skill shown by each soloist is source of much fun.    The performance should not come to an end till everyone has played a solo, and then probably a change of tune and exchange of instruments would keep the game going merrily for some time longer.

## 185.     Earth, Air, Water, Fire.

THIS is a somewhat similar game to Beasts, Birds, and Fishes. The players seat themselves in a circle. One of them throws a handkerchief at another, mentioning as he or she does so one of the four elements. If she should say "Earth," the player at whom she aimed the handkerchief must name an animal before the thrower can count ten. If she should not be quick enough to answer before the ten is swiftly counted she has to pay a forfeit. The player to whom the handkerchief was thrown has to toss it to somebody else. Should the thrower say "Air," the player to whom it is directed must name some bird or flying insect; should she say "Water," the challenge must be replied to by the name of a fish. When "Fire" is called, no answer at all must be made. Any player making a mistake in naming any of the creatures of the first three elements, or in breaking the silence when the fourth is called, has to take the handkerchief and continue the game.

## 186.  The Feather in the Sheet.

THE players hold up a sheet or cloth by the corners and sides, and blow a feather about, and keep it up in the air, never allowing it to fall in the sheet. When it does touch the sheet by any mischance, it has to be blown up again without touching it.

## 187.     A Cat's Cradle.

To make a Cat's Cradle you must take a piece of cotton about forty or fifty inches long and tie the two ends of it together, and then put your hands in this circle and hold them as far apart as they will go. You then dip one hand down and enfold a loop of the cotton round it, and then do the same with the other hand. With the middle finger of one hand you lift up this loop of cotton that encircles the opposite hand, and then with the middle finger of the other hand take up the loop on the first one, and readjust the cotton till the different lines thus formed are straight. It is then a cradle. (*Fig. 1.*) Another player is now required to "take it off." This player, with the finger and thumb of both hands, takes hold of the cotton on each side of the cradle where it crosses itself, and lifting it up first, draws it out wider, then lowers the finger and thumb tightly holding the crossed threads, and brings them up again in the centre of the surface. (*Fig. 2.*) The thumb and finger then release the cotton, when the cradle will have arrived at another stage which is something like a coverlit with a large diamond in the centre of it. The threads where they cross each other are then taken hold of with the thumbs and first fingers of the other player, and lifted up and then slipped under and through the centre of this diamond. A figure called "candles" is thus formed. (*Fig. 3.*) The little finger is next hooked round the inner line of the candle, on the side farthest from it, and the little finger of the other hand is hooked round the opposite line, the hands crossing for this manœuvre. These threads are drawn out and the thumb and first finger of each hand brought up again with them in the centre of the figure, which becomes a cradle again, only inverted. (*Fig. 4.*)

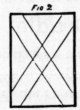
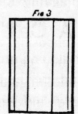
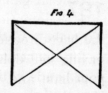

Fig 1     Fig 2     Fig 3     Fig 4

## 188.    The Stool of Penitence.

ONE player leaves the room.  All the company make some remark about the absentee, and must remember what they have said.  The absentee is then invited to enter and is motioned to sit on a stool provided for the purpose.  One of the company is chosen to inform him that somebody has made a remark about him, and repeats the purport of it, and he has to guess who was the author of it.  Should he not guess correctly he has to go out again.  The first person whose authorship of a remark is guessed correctly has then to take his or her turn of leaving the room, and afterwards of sitting on the stool of penitence and guessing the authorship of fresh remarks applied to the new player.  Supposing one says the absent player is disagreeable, another that he is charming, a third that he is clever, a fourth that he is sure to make a mark in the world, the leader who is managing the game says to him when he is called in, "One of the company says you are charming, which was it?"  Should he guess correctly, the one who passed this remark has to go out next time.  The authorship of the other remarks is abandoned when one is guessed correctly.

## 189.    The Mocking Game.

THIS is a game in which all the players are in league against one.  This one, who is a novice, is told to leave the room whilst the rest decide upon something to play at, and when they have settled what it is to be and are all playing it, they will call him in and he must guess what game it is.  Accordingly he leaves the room, but they have no intention of choosing any game, for the fun lies in quite another direction.  They call him in, and all pretend to be just leaving off doing something, and become silent and quiet.  He considers, and whatever movement he may chance to make they all imitate.  Supposing he puts his hand to his mouth, they all put their hands to their mouths; if he crosses one foot over the other, they all do the same; if he puts his hands on his knees, they all put their hands on their knees. Should he say "I am sure I cannot tell what you were playing at," they all declare simultaneously "I am sure I cannot tell what you were playing at." Of course, he soon finds out they are mocking him and laughs, and then they all laugh too, and the fun is kept up till there is no more amusement to be gained from it. To improve this game, the guesser should be required to name what the rest are doing in a word of five letters—(M.I.M.I.C.)

## 190.  The Cushion Dance.

THE Cushion Dance is a party game. A ring is formed with one player in the centre, who has a cushion (of the pillow kind) in her or his hands. All dance round and round to a pretty tune on the piano, which ceases at the end of any division of it, when the player with the cushion has to place it at the feet of whichever of the other players is preferred. If this player should be a boy, he is expected to choose a girl, and if a girl, she is expected to choose a boy. This couple then kneel down on the cushion and give each other a kiss. The first player then retires into the ring, and the newly chosen one picks up the cushion. The music is resumed, and the dance begins again. When the music stops the cushion has to be deposited at somebody else's feet, who has to kneel down on it with this new owner of it and be kissed. The third player then takes up the cushion, the second retires into the ring, the music re-commences, and the dance begins again. When everybody has been selected, and has danced round with the cushion, the game ceases.

## 191.  Charming the Mantel-piece.

THIS is a kind of thought reading. It requires a confederate. You must have only eight articles on the mantel-piece, and ask your company to fix on one of them, assuring them that your partner, who must be out of the room, will be able to tell which they have fixed upon. When they have settled which of the articles it is to be, you call your confederate in, and ask her which it is. She, or he, must know beforehand that these eight articles represent the eight personal pronouns, and that if it should be the first article that is selected, you will use the first person of the pronouns in putting your questions; if the second, you will use the second person; if the third, you will bring in mention of one of the third persons, he, she, or it. We, you, and they, are sixth, seventh, and eighth, in the row. We will say for an example that the players in the room have fixed on the third article. In putting the question, "which is it?" will be sufficient. The confederate will notice there is only one pronoun in that short sentence, and that it is the third person. She will guess that it is the third ornament. Again, supposing it is the eighth they fix on, "They have soon made up their minds," or any sentence with "they" in it, will let the confederate know it is the eighth article. (It is best to have an understanding with your partner to consider the right hand side to be the top in counting). If the sixth object should be selected, the word "we" must be introduced; if the seventh, "you" or "ye;" if the first, "I," a laugh, and "I am sure you know," will baffle detection. This secret is seldom divined.

## 192.    I Love My Love.

THIS game consists in finding words beginning with all the letters of the alphabet, one after another, with which to describe and denote particulars of your "love." The players can be seated about the room, or round a table. One begins: "I love my love with an A, because she is amiable. She took me to Antwerp and gave me apples. Her name is Annie, and she lives at Alnwick." The player seated next to this one continues, "I love my love with a B, because she is beautiful. She took me to Berwick and gave me biscuits. Her name is Beatrice, and she lives at Bradford." The third player is perhaps a girl, and goes on, "I love my love with a C, because he is careful. He took me to Cambridge and gave me chocolate. His name is Charles, and he lives at Caerphilly." If the next player should be a girl, the confession continues in the same strain, "I love my love with a D, because he is delightful. He took me to Derby and gave me damsons. His name is Dick, and he lives in Devonshire." If it should be a boy, it has to return to the presentment of a lady-love. The letters should be gone through as briskly as possible, and forfeits paid for failures to find qualities, edibles, or places with proper initials.

## 193. Consequences, & Similar Games.

In these games the players are always seated at tables, and must have pencils and pieces of paper. Taking the old favourite Consequences first, it may be briefly stated that the players must be told to write in one word, the chief characteristic of any gentleman they choose. They are then to fold the paper down so that no one can see what they have written, and each has to pass the piece written on to his or her next neighbour. Each of these new owners of the papers has to write down the name of a gentleman (if known to them all, so much the better). The papers are then folded down once more, and passed on as before, when a quality belonging to a lady is written below the last writing; and when this has been passed on, the name of a lady is added. Then, after passing on the papers every time, each time folding down and concealing what has been written, the following particulars are gradually added: where they met, what he said, what she said, the consequence, and what the world said. When the last round is finished, the folded papers are unfolded, and the writing upon them read aloud in turns, when there is sure to be a great deal of merriment arising out of the curious combinations. The following is a specimen of the result: "Clever Mr. Curtis and beautiful Miss Temple met on the Thames Embankment. He said to her, 'Is it true?' She said to him, 'How ridiculous!' The consequence was 'The coach was upset;' and the world said, 'It is never too late to mend.'"    Here is one more: "Masterful Mr. Moore met the kind-hearted Miss Smith, on the walls round York.   He said to her, 'How many horses has your father got?'   She said to him, 'Don't talk nonsense.'   The consequence was 'They were married in January;' and the world said, 'People should be careful.'"

## 194.        Reviews of Books.

THIS is done in the same way as Consequences, by putting down on slips of paper special facts and criticisms, and passing the slips on from one to another of the players, after concealing with a fold what each has written, till all have had a hand in filling up the required particulars.   For a Review, the name of an imaginary book must be the first thing written down, and when the slip with this title on it has changed hands, an alternative title must be added.   When passed on again an author's name must be written.   This is followed by an opinion on the merits of the work, and when this is accomplished and the slips passed on, another is added.   Fun is made in registering the names of persons present as having been the authors, and by giving odd names to their works, as well as by the contradictory opinions concerning them.   We will say the first chosen might be such an one as "A Fatal Consequence;" the second, or, "The Woman in Green." The sequence might then run on,—"By Miss Julia Read.—This work is full of the tenderest touches and most delicate delineations.—It is evident that it is a first attempt, and we advise the writer never to make a second."   To give another example: "A Nice Family; or, The Hermit of Piccadilly.—By Frederick St. James.—For power and pathos, for insight into the deepest emotions that surge in the innermost recesses of the human heart, we have seen nothing like this for years.—What end publishers can have in view when they issue a work of this transparent flimsiness, we cannot conceive."

Q

## 195. Spelling Bees.

SPELLING BEES were a favourite amusement a short time ago. They are
still interesting. Small prizes must be offered to competitors who
present themselves as candidates. They form a line, and a person
appointed for the purpose, beginning at the top of the line, calls out
a particular word. If the topmost candidate should spell it correctly,
a second word must be given to the second candidate; but if he
should make a mistake he must retire from the contest, and the
second person must be asked to spell the same word. If he should
fail too, he must also sit down and retire from the contest, and so on
throughout the row. Supposing the first has succeeded, and the
second likewise, another word must be given to the third candidate,
and so on. As they fail, each has to retire, till they get gradually
reduced to two. Attention is then fixed on the pair, and they are
cheered and encouraged, or laughed at, till one at last makes a mistake, when the other receives the prize. Out-of-the-way words of a
comical kind may be fixed on to puzzle and amuse the candidates, as
well as delight the spectators.

## 196. My Lady's Toilet.

THIS is a very favourite game. With the exception of one, all the
players are seated, and each takes the name of an article required in
My Lady's Toilet, such as her cloak, muff, slippers, jewellery, brushes
and combs. The one who is left out is the leader for the time being.
She stands in the centre of the room, and says her lady is going out
and wants her cloak, or any other of the items represented by the
other players that she chooses. The one who represents the article
she named has to rise and turn round, and say, "Here, my lady."
The leader, who is supposed to be my lady's maid, goes on enumer-
ating all the different articles required from time to time by her lady
in the course of her toilet. Every now and then in the flow of her
narrative talk, she mentions her lady's mirror, whereupon the whole

company has to rise and turn round. Then she goes on again, promiscuously, with mention of other items, each requiring instant recognition on the part of the players who represent it, and their rising and turning round, and the statement "Here, my lady." All this must be done briskly, to keep the company constantly rising and turning round, and the mirror must be mentioned very frequently so as to include everybody, and that the game may not "fall flat." All those who fail to turn round when the articles they represent are mentioned have to pay forfeits, which are cried at the conclusion of the game. When the maid says "My lady is dressed," all have to change seats, and the one left without one becomes the lady's maid in turn. Each player may represent two or more items of the lady's toilet to make a greater variety, if approved.

## 197.    The Thimble Game.

THE Thimble Game is suitable for very young children. They must all go out of the room whilst a thimble is put in a very conspicuous place, where everyone can easily see it without touching anything. They are then called in and told to look for it, and when they find it to make no remark, but merely sit down. After the first to see where it is has sat down, the rest go on looking about for it, and one by one, they all find it and sit down, till there is only one left looking for it. Everyone laughs to see this player so long in finding the thimble. When it is at last seen, the first person who saw it is entitled to hide it, and all the rest leave the room whilst the choice of a new and very conspicuous place is made. When one is decided upon, and the thimble once more placed in full view of all, the rest are called in and the search begins again. This game is the reverse to Hide and Seek, as a very conspicuous place, and not a secret one, is chosen for the thimble, and it does not finish when the first person finds it. Those who see it must sit down silently and give no clue as to its whereabouts to the others.

## 198. This and That.

THERE are several ways of indicating to a confederate what article people have fixed upon during his or her absence. One way is to ask the confederate when called into the room, "Is it this? Is it this?" as you point to objects that are not the one chosen, and when you indicate the right article to vary the enquiry by standing at a little distance from it, and pointing to it, with the query "Is it that?"

## 199. The Yankee Postman.

ONE player goes outside the room. He knocks at the door. The person appointed to answer the door says, "Who is there?" The player outside replies, "The Yankee Postman." He is then asked, "What with?" He replies, "A letter." The porter asks, "Who for?" The Yankee Postman names someone in the room. The porter asks, "How many stamps are there to be paid for?" The postman mentions any number he chooses. The porter then informs the person in the room who has been named, that there is a letter for him or her, and whoever this is gets up and goes out of the room to receive the imaginary letter, and pay for it with kisses according to the number of stamps demanded. The postman then comes into the room, and leaves behind him the person who came for the letter, who then becomes postman, and goes through the same conversation with the porter, and eventually names another of the company to come for another letter, and so on.

## 200. Attitudes.

Someone plays a merry tune on the piano, whilst the company run round and round the room. Suddenly the music ceases, and every player has to remain in some comical attitude till it goes on again. Those who laugh are left out of the ring. When all are out the fun is over.

## 201.   Throwing Cards into a Hat.

You place a tall hat on the ground at about six feet from your seat, and take a pack of old cards and try to throw each card into the hat. You will find only a very few will go in. When you have got through the pack, those that went in are counted and the number written down. You then vacate your seat for the next player, who in his turn tries to throw the cards into the hat. When he has exhausted the pack, the number that he has thrown in are counted and written down, and the seat vacated again, and the next player tries his prowess. He who makes the largest number of cards fall into the hat is the conqueror.

## 202.   Guessing the Height of a Hat.

This is done by asking a player to make a mark on the wall where he thinks a hat will come to. On measuring the hat against it, there is generally a great discrepancy apparent in the calculations.

## 203.      A Book on the Door.

You take a small book, or any other trifle that is handy and suitable, and announce to your comrades that you can make it remain on the door at any height they may please to choose, without touching it. You hold it pressed firmly against the door to show them what you mean. Whilst all are considering the performance, you say to one of the company, "Just hold it here, exactly as you see me doing." When this transference is quietly effected, you must walk away and seat yourself at some distance. The rest will probably remain expecting some other proceeding on your part, when you will remark, "I told you I could keep that book in any position you chose without touching it, and I have done it."

## 204. The Giant and the Dwarf.

You require three people to make a giant and a dwarf. Girls answer best. You make the giant by standing someone on a chair, and putting a long skirt over the chair, and a pair of boots or shoes just peeping from below it on the floor, to look like feet. The upper part of the figure must also be appropriately dressed to hide the junction between it and the chair. And you make the dwarf by standing the player close to a table and putting boots on her hands, which she must keep on the table to look like feet. Someone must stand hidden behind her, who must pass her hands under the dwarf's arms, so as to look as though they belong to her, whereas her own are in the boots. The rest of the dwarf's dress must be attended to, to make her look completely clad and finished at her feet on the table. You then admit the rest of the company. The giant talks and moves her head and arms about, and the dwarf moves her boots about on the table to draw attention to them, and the person hidden behind it waves her hands occasionally, and altogether there is a very comical piece of amusement; and when seen for the first time it is generally much enjoyed. If you can make a speech like a showman it will be still more entertaining. The showman might say something of this sort: "There was once a showman who had the Duke of Wellington and Napoleon Buonaparte in his show, and when anyone asked him which was which, he used to say, 'Whichever you please, my pretty little dear.' Now I cannot say the same if you ask me which is which. This, of course, is the giant" (and he must point to the dwarf), "and this is the dwarf" (pointing to the giant).

## 205. Recent Engagements.

A LARGE circle is formed with seats. When all the players are seated, each player whispers to the one on his or her left the name of a gentleman, and when this has been done by the whole circle, each player whispers to the one on the right of him or her the name of a lady. When this has gone the round, the first player then remarks that she or he is happy to announce the engagement of Mr. So-and-so, mentioning the name whispered to her on the one hand, to Miss So-and-so, mentioning the lady whispered to her on the other hand. Perhaps it is an engagement between a very little boy and an old lady that is thus indicated, or that of a stout old gentleman to a tiny girl. It is the incongruities of the various engagements that make the fun. In some circles the form is, "I publish the banns of marriage between," and then follow the names in the cross-ways manner given.

## 206.    Creeping into a Bottle.

THIS is a game that partakes of the nature of a trick, or amusing deception. You ask the assembled children if they have ever seen anyone creep into a bottle, and you elaborately explain that you mean quite an ordinary bottle, a common black wine bottle with a narrow neck, and that you know how it is done. It is a bit of fun that can only be played once in the course of an evening, because no one can be astonished twice by the statement. When it is settled that you are to perform this wonderful feat, you get a bottle of any kind, and place it in the middle of the room, and ask the company to form a circle round it, and keep their eyes upon it. When a ring round it is thus made, you leave the room for a minute, and on re-opening the door you creep into the circle, straight up to the bottle, on all fours. You then get up and remark coolly that it is an extremely simple process; no more than that; and that anybody could do it who liked to try. The company soon see the joke.

## 207.                         Rabbits.

THIS is another game that is to a similar extent a delusion and a snare. The players are instructed by the person who sets the game going, to stand in a circle, then stoop or kneel down, and put the first and second fingers of both hands on the floor in a smaller ring, so that all the fingers are touching. When the circle of fingers is adjusted, the one conducting the game whispers to the player next to him, " Do you know how to play rabbits ? " As he does not know, he replies to that effect, and is then told to ask his neighbour on the other side of him. When this neighbour also replies in the negative, he is told to whisper the same question to the player on the other side. When the query and reply have gone all round the circle, the person who has started the game remarks, " Do none of you know how to play rabbits ? Neither do I, so we can't play it." Upon which the players resume their upright positions, generally midst much laughter.

## 208. The Hot Penny.

You place a row of pence on the table, and announce that if anyone likes to hold one of them in his hand during your absence from the room, you will tell him which he has so held on your return. He must be told to hold it tight all the time. When he has put it down again and calls you into the room, you take up penny after penny and pretend to feel it carefully. When you come to one warm, you tell him that is it.

## 209. A Trick with a Penny.

You announce that you can tell which hand has a penny in it. You produce a penny and tell your comrade to take it and hold it up above his head. You turn your back while he does so. After a few minutes' delay, you tell him to put both hands clenched upon the table and you will tell which has the penny in it. You will notice the one he has held above his head is much whiter than the other, and guess accordingly.

## 210.  Jack and Jill.

To entertain very young children put two pieces of paper, about
the size of a postage stamp, upon your two first fingers. You must
slightly wet the paper to make it stick on. Then put your two
fingers with the paper on them close together on the edge of the
table, and dance them about. After a time you say, "Fly away
Jack," and withdraw one finger and substitute your middle finger for
it; then "Fly away Jill," and remove the other first finger and
substitute your other middle finger for it. You then say, "Come
again Jack," and bring back the first finger with the paper still on it;
then "Come again Jill," and bring back the other, simultaneously
removing the middle fingers.

## 211.  The Spelling Game.

THIS is an ingenious game in which every player has three lives, or
chances. When seated in a circle, or semi-circle, the first player
mentions a letter as the beginning of a word, and it is the business
of the rest, successively, to add letter after letter to it, one at a time,
each successive player keeping the word unfinished as long as
possible. When a letter is added to a word which completes it, the
person in whose hands it comes to an end loses a life. The first
player then starts another letter, and, as before, in the order in
which they sit, the rest add another one to it till a word is spelt out
that admits of no addition. Every letter added must always be
part of the proper formation of a word, and not an odd one that
does not belong to any. When there is any suspicion that the letter
is not used legitimately, the person adding it may be challenged,
and required to name the word he is spelling with this letter in it.
To give examples :— The first player mentions any letter he likes,
say B; the next, thinking of "Bay-tree," says A; the next adds S,
thinking of "Basket;" the next, not having either of these things in his

mind, says T, meaning to spell "Bastile," if challenged; the next, having no idea of this, says I; the next, thinking of "Bastion," says O. It occurs to someone in the circle that there is no word of which the first six letters are B. A. S. T. I. O., who therefore cries out, "I challenge that word." The player who added the O explains that it was "Bastion" he meant to spell; whereupon the challenger has lost one of his three lives. We will say the first player then says P; the next says I; the next, not wanting to lose a life, or one of his three chances, by adding a letter that would make pie, or pip, or pig, or any short complete word, adds B; the next, unable to think of any word of which this might form part, but "Pibroch," says R; the next, feeling equally limited, gives out O; the next, having no alternative says C; and the last has to make it complete with H, and thus loses a life. It will be observed that a player loses a life in three ways; he may mention a letter that is not a component part of a word; challenge another player who is not at fault; or be obliged to finish up a word with its final letter, because he cannot think of another word into which to convert it. We will suppose the first player next takes C; the second, thinking of "Coal," says O; the third, thinking of "Comma," says M; the next, thinking of many words in which this letter is doubled, says another M; the next, having "Common" in view, says O; the next, determined not to lose a life by letting the word conclude with him says D; no one challenging, the next continues with I; and the word being thus far advanced, the rest can only complete it, letter by letter, as "Commodious," and the player who has to say S loses a life. It is not possible to add ly, or ness, to the word, because it is already a complete one, when it has arrived at "Commodious," and it is a rule that whenever a word arrives at any stage of completeness, it is finished. As each player loses his three lives he retires from the game, till there are only two left, when it soon comes to a close. Someone should be appointed to keep count of losses of lives, if there should be a large number of players. To give a final example :—The first letter chosen may be L ; the second player may add U, thinking if challenged, he would spell "Lump ;" the next, feeling sure of plenty of words beginning with lum, says M ; the next has some such word as "Luminary" in view, and says I ; the next feels safe with adding N ; another trying to lengthen out the word adds I ; and, now the assortment of available words narrowing, the rest can only add F. E. R. O. U. S. consecutively in turns, and the one to whom the S falls loses a life.

## 212.  Cross Questions and Crooked Answers.

THIS old-fashioned game consists in asking a question of one person, and giving the reply of another person to a different one, thus crossing the questions and replies.  It is necessary that the players should be seated in a circle, and sufficiently near to one another for whispers not to be overheard.  One player, we will suppose it is a young lady, begins by whispering a question to the one seated next to her, who replies also in a whisper, and then turns and asks another question of the person seated on the other side of her.  This arrangement goes on all round the circle.  The first player then begins to narrate aloud that a question was put to her, and she gives the question that was asked her by the person on her left, and the answer that was given to her own question by the person on her right.  To give an example.  "The question was put to me, 'Do you like music ?' and the answer was, 'Yes, fried.'"  The second player would go on to say, "The question was put to me, 'Do you like fish ?' and the answer was, 'Not without the banjo.'"  The third player would continue in some such way as "The question was put to me, 'Do you like nigger songs ?' and the answer was, 'Yes, covered with diamonds.'"  The fourth would explain this crooked answer by telling that the question was put to her, "Was the prima donna splendidly dressed?" and the answer she received would open up a fresh wonderment by further crookedness.

## 213. Ariel's Nose.

ARIEL'S NOSE is a simple alphabetical game. All the players may seat themselves or stand in a semi-circle. The first commences by saying that Ariel's nose has some peculiarity beginning with the letter A: "Ariel's nose is aquiline," or "Ariel's nose is adequate"— for a little fun to be introduced is better—and the next player has to make a similar statement of a peculiarity belonging to the same feature, and the next, till the whole semi-circle has assigned some quality, or condition, to it that begins with A. The first player then recommences by assigning some quality that begins with B, to Ariel's nose; it is broad, bent, or beautiful, or anything else that begins with B. When this letter has gone the round of the players, the first begins again with C, saying "Ariel's nose is clumsy," or curious, or childish, or anything commencing with C. Then the round is made again with D, and Ariel's nose is declared to be disfigured, decent, dignified, disgraceful, or anything beginning with D, till the semi-circle is completed once more. They go on to E, and the nose is elegant, emblematic, or embossed, and so on. All the letters of the alphabet are thus used to describe Ariel's nose, in rotation. Those who cannot think of a suitable descriptive word when their turns come, have to pay forfeits, which are cried afterwards.

## 214. Buff says Buff to all His Men.

THIS is one of the games in which laughing is attended with the penalty of a forfeit. The players are all seated, when the first one takes a stick, or poker, and rapping on the ground with it so as to command attention, gives the following message as solemnly as he can :—

> Buff says Buff to all his men,
> And I say Buff to you again ;
> And Buff he never laughs, nor smiles,
> In spite of all your cunning wiles,
> But keeps his face, with a very good grace,
> And carries his staff to the very next place.

He then passes his stick to another player, who has to go through the same form. When a player laughs he must pay a forfeit. The game goes on till everyone has been Buff, and then the forfeits are cried. Of course, everyone tries to make everyone else laugh, either by witty remarks, or antics, or grimaces.

## 215.    The Match in the Flour.

You put some flour on a plate and pat it into a square, then stick a match into the middle of the top of it, like a little flag-staff, then take a knife, and each player must cut a piece off the pile of flour in turn, without disturbing the match. The first to let the match fall nas to pay a forfeit.

## 216.    Choosing Three Flowers.

This is to amuse very young children. A player has to choose three flowers, and the person playing with him names three children in his mind. The one who has chosen the flowers is then asked "What would you do with the first one ?" The other replies, according to his fancy, that he would wear it, or put it in water, or throw it in the fire, or anything that he thinks suitable. The one who has chosen children, then announces the name of the child he has thought of. For example, the flower chooser may have thought of the lily; the child chooser may have thought of his brother. When asked what he would do with it, the first player might say, having in his mind the lily, "wear it in my buttonhole," when the other would cry "you would wear my brother in your buttonhole." And so on through the three flowers, when the incongruity of putting an aunt in water, or a sister in a glass vase, or throwing an uncle into the fire, affords amusement to very little folks. Older ones play it with the proviso that one of the answers must be "next my heart." To every flower the question comes "Where will you put it?"

## 217.  The Hatchet.

THIS mysterious matter may be investigated either in an ordinary circle of little players, or when there is a party of them assembled round a table. To begin the fun, you must take up a spoon if at table, or a paper knife, or ruler, or similar article, if elsewhere, and offer it to your neighbour, who must be instructed to ask, "What's this?" You reply mysteriously and confidentially, "a hatchet." Your neighbour must then turn to the person on the other side of him or her, who must ask the same question, to which your neighbour must give the same reply that you gave her. This question and whispered reply, and the article, go on from one to another all round the circle. When the spoon or paper knife, or whatever it may be, after completing the round, returns to you, your neighbour must be instructed to ask, "Did you buy it?" You shake your head, in deep silence. The same question and the mute reply go round the circle again, as well as the article. On returning to you, when you begin to send the so called hatchet round again, your neighbour must ask, "Did you steal it?" You place your first finger on your lips, and glancing about timorously, murmur "Hush!" This query and murmured reply also go round the circle. Your neighbour is then instructed to ask, "What is it for?" You then draw your finger round your neck, and make a noise as of decapitation, rendered according to fancy, but as comically as possible, which generally brings out a hearty laugh, which is repeated as the catastrophe is illustrated by the different players.

## 218.       Charades.

THERE is an immense amount of amusement to be found in the acting of Charades, under almost any conditions. The company divide into two parties. The first party to perform, chosen by lot or agreement, chooses a word that appears to them easy of illustration. We will suppose they choose "inhabitant." In the first place they might represent someone arriving at an *inn*, and being received by the landlord; in the second, they might show a lady in a *habit*, perhaps having it mended; in the third, an observer watching the proceedings of an *ant*, with a magnifying glass; and in the fourth, a very old person as the oldest *inhabitant*. Should the opposite side guess correctly what has been represented, the first side becomes the audience, and takes its turn at guessing. We will suppose the second party settle to represent Kingfisher. In their first scene, they might show a King seated on a throne, receiving ambassadors; in their next, a man fishing; in their last, a museum of wild birds, in it one of which must be a Kingfisher. In one way of playing charades, the particular syllable portrayed must be introduced into the dialogue in each scene, and the whole word into the final one. Some players think this gives the clue too clearly, and avoid all mention of the word. It should be settled before commencing to play which plan shall be adopted. Should either side not guess what has been intended, it loses its turn, and the other side has another.

## 219.       The Huntsman.

THIS game is very much like "The sea is agitated," but it makes a pleasant variety. There is the same double row of chairs required, that provides a seat for all the players but one. All the players are given the names of parts of a huntsman's gear-gun, belt, flask, coat, cap, powder, dog, &c. When all are seated, the huntsman walks round the company and calls first one and then the other, by their assumed names. When the first one rises to his call, he has to take hold of the coat-tail of the huntsman; and as the rest are called, they take hold of the coat or skirt of the player before him or her. When all are called and are walking in the procession, the huntsman begins to run round the empty chairs as fast as he can, all following in his wake. Suddenly he cries "Bang," and seats himself, and the rest have to do the same. The one left without a seat becomes the huntsman.

## 220.     Judge and Jury.

ONE of the party is selected to be Judge. The rest arrange themselves into two lines, and seat themselves opposite to each other. Each one has to remember who is exactly opposite to him, because when the Judge puts a question to anyone, it is not the person addressed who is to answer, but the person exactly opposite to him. The Judge then begins to question either of the players on any subject he chooses: "So-and-so, do you write letters on blotting paper?" The one addressed must remain silent, but the person opposite to him must reply before the Judge can count ten, or he loses his seat and has to be the Judge, and the first Judge takes his place. There are some restrictions as to answers. They must never contain less than two words, and they must not have the words "yes, no, black, or white" in them. These limitations make this game more complicated than it looks at first sight.

## 221.    A Simple Alphabet Game.

WHEN seated, the first player states "Ann ate an apple," or anything else in which there are but four words, and all of them begin with A. The second, "Bella bakes bad bread," or states some other fact in four words beginning with B. The next player goes on to C: "Cook cuts capital capers," or "Caroline clarifies cold coffee," or any other four words beginning with C. Some of the consonants present difficulties that make this little game more entertaining than it looks at first sight. "Jolly Julia jokes judiciously;" but X, Y and Z, are not quite so easily dismissed.

## 222. Rhyming Words.

THIS is another simple game for very young players. One begins, "I am thinking of a word to rhyme with Bun." The guessers ask indirectly, "Is it something to shoot with?" And if the answer is "Yes," then they bring out their guess more directly—"Gun." Thus, it will be seen that guessers do not say the word thought of till they have described its use or meaning. The next player goes on, "I am thinking of a word to rhyme with Hog." The guessers may ask, thinking of Dog, "Does it bark?" but the answer may be "No." Then they must guess again, such as "Does it lie still?" If "log" is the word, it is acknowledged, and the next player states that he has thought of a word to rhyme with something else.

## 223. Crossed or Not Crossed.

THIS is a game in which mystification is the chief feature. When the mystery is explained or correctly guessed, the fun is over. A pair of scissors is required for its performance, and the larger they are the more conspicuous and suitable they will be found. The person in the secret sees that everyone is seated. He then opens the scissors wide, and passes them to the next person, saying "Crossed," and motions to him to pass them on. The next person does so, and then the next, till the complete round of the players has been made. The leader then takes the scissors again and passes them round as before, only they are closed this time, and he says "uncrossed," as he does so. When they have been all round the company, he puts a finger into one of the loops of the scissors, leaving them wide open and depending from his finger, saying "crossed." And this passing

S

of the scissors round the circle goes on, always slightly altering the manner of holding them, so as to make the players fancy the secret lies in the manner they are passed. Every now and then, the leader declares someone is "wrong." As this person has, probably, observed all the details that were apparent to him, he cannot tell in what particular he has not followed the leader's example. The explanation lies in the fact that when the leader passes the scissors, saying "crossed," he has crossed his own feet, and when he passes them saying "uncrossed," he has uncrossed them. When he calls out "wrong," it is because a player has said "crossed" when his feet were uncrossed, and *vice versa*.

## 224.   How do you like your Neighbour?

ALL the company must be seated for this game, except the "man out." He fixes upon any he pleases to ask, "How do you like your neighbour?" If the person he asks should reply, "very well," or "very much," all the players instantly change their seats by moving into the next one nearest to their right hand, when the interlocutor tries to secure one of the seats. Should he reply "not at all," or "not much," the interlocutor goes on to ask "Whom would you prefer?" The two he names (one for either side of him) must rise and rush to the two seats immediately vacated by the two neighbours he dislikes, and in the confusion of the transit, the "man out" has to try and get one of the four seats left momentarily unoccupied. This is not always difficult, as the entanglement of the players is often so considerable that they run into each other, which causes a laughing delay that enables the "man out" to slip into one of their seats. The player left without a seat then takes the place of the "man out," and asks anyone he pleases, "How do you like your neighbour?" If he likes them everyone moves one place. If he says he does not like them, the same question is put to him, "Whom do you prefer?" And on these players being named, those on either side of him must get up and try to reach the seats of the players preferred, before he can install himself in either of them, and, in like haste, the two named must run to the seats vacated by the two neighbours. The person to whom the questions are addressed only moves one seat to the right, like the rest, when he approves of his neighbours. When he states that he does not like them and would prefer two others, he sits still and does not budge.

## 225. Overheard Conversation.

Two players privately agree upon a word having two or more meanings. To do this they need not leave the room, but one can write it on a scrap of paper and pass it to the other. The rest of the party then listen, whilst these two enter into conversation in which they speak of the meaning of the word they have chosen, without mentioning it. When a member of the party thinks he has guessed it, he may join in the conversation till he finds he is mistaken, when he must fall out of it again. We will say the two commencing the game take the word "Fair." They might talk of the number of people that were at some imaginary fair, taking care not to mention the word, and allude to the shows, giants, dwarfs, gilt gingerbread, clowns, tents, flags, and bands; and then pass on to remarks in which the word was treated as meaning a railway "Fare," and dwell upon its costliness or cheapness; and then take another turn as though it related to complexions, and after that to dealings.. By this time the company will be, probably, completely mystified. Every time any player fancies he has found the word he joins in. His remarks are generally so wide of the mark as serve only to add to the puzzle. Should anyone guess the word correctly, it is his turn to think of another, and to converse about it with any partner he may choose. Should no one guess it, it must be "given up," and the same two think of another word, and converse about it as before. We will give, as an example, the word "Place." This may be talked about as a holiday resort lately visited, or about to be visited; or as a situation vacant, or to be vacated; or as a fish (plaice,) enjoyed at some meal, or caught upon some occasion. Or, we will take the word "Deer." Here there may be talk of parks, and herds, and shooting parties in the Highlands and elsewhere, and the expense of living (dear), or of some article of attire or luxury that has been purchased. The choice of a fresh word each time makes the game ever new.

## 226.    How to redeem Forfeits.

THERE are so many games that are played under pain of penalties, by which little articles of trifling value are forfeited till they are redeemed by the performance of certain ceremonies, that it has been thought well to draw up a list of the peculiar actions that, from time immemorial, have been considered suitable for the purpose. There is a proper form for the crying of forfeits that must invariably be used. A lady seats herself in a chair, and one of the other players kneels before her with his or her face so hidden in the lady's lap that the articles held up over his or her head, in the ceremonious discharge of the adjudication, cannot be seen. The lady, holding up an article that has been forfeited, says, "Here is a pretty thing, and a very pretty thing, and what must be done to the owner of this very pretty thing?" The person kneeling must ask, "Is it a lady or a gentleman?" On being told, he mentions a penance. This is performed by the owner of the article, to whom it is then returned; and the crying goes on till all the forfeits are returned to their owners, after the various sins of omission and commission, of which they were tokens, have been duly expiated. Some of these penalties are of interesting antiquity.

1. Measure six yards of love ribbon. The owner must take hold of somebody else's hands and stretch them out as far apart as possible. This will bring their faces close together, when he

must give his partner a kiss. He opens his arms again still holding her hands, and when their faces come together as before there must be another kiss. This has to be done six times, or as often as the "crier" likes to enforce.

2. To spell a live mouse-trap with three letters. (C. A. T.)
3. To stand on a newspaper with any other member of the party without touching them. (This is done by passing the open paper under a door, and one standing on it outside the door, the other inside.)
4. To stand on five legs. (This is done by putting one foot on a chair.)
5. To spell pepper with two letters. (K. N.)
6. To look at all the other players, bow to the wittiest, kneel to the prettiest, and kiss the one he loves best.
7. To go into the four corners of the room, dance in one, sing in another, laugh in the third, and cry in the other.
8. To say all the letters of the alphabet in these syllables,—ab, c, def, g, hijklm, n, op, q, rstu, v, w, xyz.
9. Repeat "She sells sea shells " four times without a mistake.
10. Go into the middle of the room and say :
    "Kimo nairy, kilta cairy,
    Kimo nairy kimo ;
    Strim, strum, strammadiddle,
    Lully bolly gig,
    With a rig dom bully diggy kimo."
11. To stand on one leg whilst the company count ten, which they will do very slowly.
12. To weigh one of the other players six times. This is for boys. They stand back to back and hook their arms into one another's, and then by one bending forward he lifts the other off his feet, and when the other in his turn bends forward, the first mentioned is lifted in a similar manner.

13. Say "just like me" to everything that is said. Example : "I came to a house," (the owner of the forfeit must say, "just like me.") "I went upstairs," ("just like me.") "I came downstairs," ("just like me.") "I went to the stable," ("just like me,") "and there I saw a donkey,"—to which he must add, "just like me," amidst the general laughter.

14. To crawl round the room on all fours.

15. To ask a riddle that no one can answer.

16. To sing a song that nobody knows.

17. To show the assembly something that has never been seen by mortal eye before (the kernal of a nut).

18. To bite an inch off a candle, or poker (that is at the distance of an inch).

19. Draw a pig on a piece of paper whilst blindfolded.

20. Draw a cat just as it is leaving the room (the tail only).

21. Play a tune with a wet cork on the side of a glass of water.

22. Say what the following letters spell. Ba-cka-che, and So-met-i-mes. (Back-ache and Sometimes.)

23. Kiss someone rabbit fashion. This is done by both players taking an end of the same piece of cotton in their mouths, and nibbling it up till their two faces come so close together that they can kiss.

24. To say " The House that Jack built " in French, or grandiloquent English : " This is the structure that John erected," &c. Or give the American version of "Sing a song of sixpence," beginning " Sing a song of dollars, a pocket full of grass, five-and-thirty swallows, baked in apple sass." Or give some other interesting recitation.

# OTHER BOOKS AVAILABLE
# FROM PRYOR PUBLICATIONS

---

## Don't: A Manual of Mistakes and Improprieties more or less prevalent in Conduct and Speech. By CENSOR.

*UNMUTILATED and with the additional matter.*
*The only Authorised and COMPLETE Edition.* £4.00

---

## English As She Is Spoke: OR A JEST IN SOBER EARNEST.

*"Excruciatingly funny"*—THE WORLD. £3.75

---

## CHRISTMAS ENTERTAINMENTS

Illustrated with many diverting cuts—a reprint of the very amusing and scarce 1740 edition, an original copy of which would now command more than twice its weight in gold. £3.00

---

## Why Not Eat Insects? "Them insecs eats up every blessed green thing that do grow, and us farmers starves."

"Well, eat *them*, and grow fat!" £3.75

---

## A PLAIN COOKERY BOOK FOR THE WORKING CLASSES *from an original copy published in 1861.*
## BY CHARLES ELMÉ FRANCATELLI
### LATE MAÎTRE D'HÔTEL AND CHIEF COOK TO HER GRACIOUS MAJESTY QUEEN VICTORIA

It contains recipes such as "Baked Bullocks Hearts," "Treacle Pudding," "Giblet Pie," "Sheep Pluck," "Cow Meal Broth" and "Rice Gruel, a Remedy for Relaxed Bowles." £3.75

CHILDREN'S SINGING GAMES

1894

This facsimile of Children's Singing Games, first published in 1894, will also appeal very much to adults in their own right.

There are eight games with words, music and instructions on playing, together with an explanation of their origins. Most striking are the superb Line illustrations.

This enchanting book gives a refreshing glimpse of part of our heritage almost forgotten about in this age of alternative children's entertainments.

A second series will be publishes in due course.

*Price* **£8.00**

---

"*Buy a fine Singing Bird?*"

# Old London Cries

A quality reprint of an 1885 edition with over 140 pages of informative and interesting reading, together with over 50 woodcuts depicting various street traders of London from the seventeenth century.

*Price*
**£7.95**

*ALL POST FREE*
A full list of our publications sent free on request.

**PRYOR PUBLICATIONS**
75 Dargate Road, Yorkletts, Whitstable , Kent CT5 3AE
Tel. & Fax: (0227) 274655

# *Three Important Drill Books.*

## THE "PORTLAND" PHYSICAL DRILL
### FOR GIRLS AND INFANTS,
*Being Movements to Music for all Young Children.*     Bound in Cloth, Price 1/8 net.
### By JENNETT HUMPHREYS.

I N this book a New Method appears which explains itself at a glance, offering no difficulties whatever. A second set of movements has been added on each page of letterpress, with the title of "second usage." Concerning the March arranged to terminate each Lesson, it can be affirmed that it will give remarkable enjoyment and recreation. The variety in it of sportive steps ensure that it will never become stale and unprofitable; and should it be desired to continue any step for a longer period than is set down, it is only necessary to repeat the division of the music in which it occurs.

## PHYSICAL EXERCISES FOR BOYS AND GIRLS,
With Music, and Illustrated with 80 Diagrams.     Bound in Cloth, Price 2/6.
### By the late WINIFRED WILSON.

T HE new Code, requiring a portion of time to be alloted in school hours to Physical Exercises, recognises the supreme importance of a free use of all the limbs and muscles as a means of acquiring a healthy body and a healthy mind. These Exercises are an important aid to the acquirement of knowledge, in so far as it brings the body to a condition in which the brain is able to perform its functions with the utmost ease and with the best results. With this fact before us, the Exercises are so arranged in the present volume that every part of the body shall partake of alternate exercise, so that no portion of it may be either neglected or unduly developed at the expense of the rest.

National and other well-known Airs have been chosen as being most likely to please all those who are concerned.

## THE "FARRINGDON" MUSICAL DRILL
FOR INFANTS.    With and Without Apparatus.    Bound in Cloth Boards, Price 2/6.
### By the late WINIFRED WILSON.

#### EXTRACT FROM INTRODUCTION.
"As it appeared desirable that some new movements should be suggested for the drill of infants in schools, I have arranged the following series, and hope that this new Musical Drill will give the satisfaction to Her Majesty's Inspectors that will ensure the highest Government grant to those schools that adopt it. . . . There are twenty-four exercises without apparatus. A selection of twelve of them is sufficient for daily use, as the whole of them would take too much time, as well as overtax the strength of the children. As the first exercises are arranged to have no apparatus whatever, they will be found useful for frequent use between changes of occupation, between lessons, or for any short intervals. The second portion of the work consists of twelve exercises, or drills, arranged for the purpose of making fresh use, with new movements, of such minor apparatus as most schools have now in use, or in their possession."

List of Calisthenic Apparatus, including May-Pole, free on application to
### A. BROWN & SONS, Ltd., 26, 27, 28, & 29, SAVILE STREET, HULL.

LONDON: A. BROWN & SONS, Ltd., 5, Farringdon Avenue, E.C. And at HULL and YORK.

BROWNS' SCHOOL SERIES.

Price 2/6. Net 1/11; post free for 2/2 net from A. B. & S., Ltd., Hull.

# DELIGHTFUL DITTIES

## FOR INFANT SCHOOLS,

**By TOM PIERCE COWLING,** *Author of the " Young Songster."*

THIS Book forms a complete Song Book for all classes and wants of the Infant Schoolroom. Its special features are:—(1) The songs are pretty, tuneful, easy, and original. (2) The words are such as children can enjoy and understand. Some rather advanced songs are given for the Standard children.

## PART I.

### Morning Songs.

Come, rouse ye.
See the merry, merry morn.

### Evening Songs.

Now at last the merry sun.
Do you know how many stars.
On the goods that are not thine.
Now the day is over.

### Sacred Songs.

Maker of all things.
Easter flow'rs are blooming bright.
When the weary day is ended.
Hark! the bells are sweetly knelling.

## PART II.

### March Songs.

Dear little Snowdrop lift up your head
Gaily singing, tra, la, la.
Go up higher, sturdy schoolboy.
We are soldiers gay.

### Kindergarten Songs.

Over one, under one, over one again.
We are builders building high.
Peep within our little box.
On that frame ten balls we see.

### Ring Songs.

Join with us and form a merry ring.
Let us dance and let us sing.

### Finger Plays.

I've eight white sheep all fast asleep.
Oh! where is little Boy Blue?

### Drill Songs.

The time has come for us to drill.

## PART III.

### Old Friends with New Faces.

How many miles to Babyland?
Little Jack Horner.
Little Bo Peep has lost her sheep.
Old Mother Hubbard.
Little Miss Muffett.
Mary, Mary, quite contrary.
Sing a song of sixpence.
The North wind doth blow.
Twinkle, twinkle, little star.
Rock-a-bye, baby, on a tree top.

## PART IV.

### Doll Ditties.

My doll has gone to-day to school.
My doll is one year old to-day.
In her little cradle.
Good Morning, dear dolly.
Dear little Baby, looking so wise.
Past eight o'clock.
Here we come with our dollies dear.

## PART V.

### Action Songs.

Pretty Puss, one moonlight night.
If I were a little bird.
Pretty bird, as on you wing.
Tell me not of towns and cities.
Bessie had a pussy cat.
" Will you walk into my parlour?"
In a crack near the cupboard.
Now the time has come for drill.
Four jolly children, all of a row.
A pound is yellow, and so bright.
At twelve o'clock 'tis noon we say.
A sweet little face at the window.
I am a blacksmith stout and strong.
My Master grinds an organ.
I'll be a jolly blacksmith.

LONDON: A. BROWN & SONS, Ltd., 5, Farringdon Avenue, E.C. And at HULL and YORK

Price 2/6.  Net 1/11; post free for 2/3 net from A. B. & S., Ltd., Hull.  QUITE NEW.

# THE "YOUNG SONGSTER."

## By TOM PIERCE COWLING, Author of "Delightful Ditties."

THIS complete Song Book should at once commend itself to all Teachers.  It contains 61 Sweet Songs, with Piano Accompaniment and Sol-Fa.  The Music all through the Book is **quite original,** and in many cases the words are also.  A glance at the Contents given below will at once show that ample provision is made for all times and needs of the Infant Department.

## PART I.

### Songs of Prayer and Praise.

The Morning Comes.
The Dawn of Day.
Day by Day we Magnify Thee.
Soldiers of Christ Arise.
Summer Suns are Glowing.
Jesu, Tender Shepherd.
Evening Hymn.
The Day was Done.
Little Knees should Lowly Bend.
The King of Love my Shepherd is.
The Message.
Hark! the Merry Bells are Ringing.
Hushed was the Evening Hymn.
Come, let us Hail the Dawning.

## PART II.

### Recreation, Drill, and Marching Songs.

Little Cherry Blossom.
The time has come for Exercise.
Raise your Hands.
Imitation Song.
The Clock.
Do your Best.
One, Two, Three.
The Boy and the Wren.
Strive to Learn.
The Merry Sailor.

## PART III.

### LULLABY SONGS.

In my Soft White Bed.
Good-Night.
Wynken, Blynken, and Nod.
Dolly's Lullaby.

## PART IV.

Little Drops of Water.
The Merry Mice.
Waken Daisies.
Ding, Dong, Bell.
The Mill.
Among the Hay.
To a River.
A Song of Summer.
Waiting to Grow.
Where did you come from.
Tell me what the Mill doth Say.
Good - Night and Good-Morning.
Run, Little Rivulet.
The Birdie's Bell.
The Little Boy's Wash.

## PART V.

### SPECIAL SONGS.

Red Letter Days.
Little White Lily.
The Fairy Ship.
The Doll's Party.
A Song of May.
A Song of Summer.
A Song of Autumn.
A Song of Winter.
A Cricket Song.

### ACTION SONGS and GAMES.

The Miller's Song.
The Soldier's Song.
The Young Astronomer.
The Lost Doll.
The Cricket's Chirp.
A Little Ship.
Making Butter.
Our Donkey.
The Frogs at School.

LONDON: A. BROWN & SONS, Limited, Publishers, 5, Farringdon Avenue, E.C.  And at HULL and YORK

T

## SPECIMEN PAGE from

### Y. A. PRIMER.—I.

Directions for Colouring with Browns' No. 250 Y. A. Crayons.

RAT.—*Lightly* with Brown.          BOX.—Green.
JACK.—*Lightly* with Red.  Red Cheeks.  Red Nose.
Hair—Black.

The pin he un-did,

Up went the lid,

Out shot a man!

Off the rat ran.

## BROWNS'
## Young Artists'
# PRIMERS

These little Primers have been compiled by an Infant School Mistress, who has had considerable experience in teaching three and four year olds. Her work in the reading lessons has been so successful that the Publishers of these small books can confidently recommend them as suitable for either large or small classes. Most of the words are in one syllable, and, as far as possible, the lines are made to rhyme.

Illustrations appear on nearly every page, and these can be coloured by the scholars, under the guidance of the teacher.

Each book contains 16 pages, printed on specially prepared paper, in sight-preserving green ink, and sewn in a stout printed wrapper.

LONDON: A. BROWN & SONS, Ltd., 5, Farringdon Avenue, E.C.  And at HULL and YORK.

## BROWNS' YOUNG ARTIST'S SERIES.

### PACKETS 3, 4, 5, and 6.

# COLOURED DRAWING COPIES

### For INFANTS and STANDARD I.

**The most popular article ever introduced into Infant Schools. Specimens free. Designed for Drawing with Coloured Crayons. Price 2/- net each packet.**

| | |
|---|---|
| **PACKET 3** COLOURED. | This consists of a packet of 32 Cards, designs all different, printed in 6 colours, of Animals and Common Objects. It will be found to be probably the most pleasing "occupation" that has yet been introduced, as no child is to be found with a distaste for drawing, especially in colours. In the author's own school the children can draw these copies from memory. |
| **PACKET 4** COLOURED. | The Copies after same style as packet 3 in character of designs. There are the same number of Cards in the packet. |
| **PACKET 5** COLOURED. | The designs in this packet are Geometric patterns. There are the same number of Cards in the packet. |
| **PACKET 6** COLOURED. | The designs are similar in style to packets 3 and 4. This packet contains chiefly animals and subjects suitable for connective lessons. |

**Browns' Young Artist's Box of Solid Crayons,** for use with any or all of the above, contains the 7 exact colours used in printing these Cards. Price 1½d.; to Schools, 1/- net per doz. boxes; per post, 1/4 per doz. Boxes are now made of Tin.

**Browns' Young Artist's Crayon Holder,** for using up small pieces of Crayons, made of silvered brass. 5/5 per gross net.

**Browns' Young Artist's Drawing Book** is the only book appropriate for use with the Drawing Cards, they being ruled to fit the squares to a nicety, which is an essential point. Price per doz., 9d. net; post free, 1/- per doz.

**Browns' Box of Coloured Chalks for the Blackboard.** Containing 100 sticks of the 7 colours required for the above. Price 2/- net; post free 2/6 net.

**LONDON: A. BROWN & SONS, Limited, Publishers, 5, Farringdon Avenue, E.C. And at HULL and YORK.**